THE AEROSPACE
ENVIRONMENT

THE WYKEHAM SCIENCE SERIES

General Editors:

PROFESSOR SIR NEVILL MOTT, F.R.S.
Emeritus Cavendish Professor of Physics
University of Cambridge

G. R. NOAKES
Formerly Senior Physics Master
Uppingham School

The aim of the Wykeham Science Series is to introduce the present state of the many fields of study within science to students approaching or starting their careers in University, Polytechnic, or College of Technology. Each book seeks to reinforce the link between school and higher education, and the main author, a distinguished worker or teacher in the field, is assisted by an experienced sixth form schoolmaster.

THE AEROSPACE ENVIRONMENT

Tom Beer
University of Ghana

 WYKEHAM PUBLICATIONS (LONDON) LTD
(A MEMBER OF THE TAYLOR & FRANCIS GROUP)
LONDON & WINCHESTER
1976

First published 1976 by Wykeham Publications (London) Ltd.

Cover illustration—Auroral display.   (Photograph by G. Lamprecht.)

ISBN 0 85109 021 4

Printed in Great Britain by Taylor & Francis (Printers) Ltd. Rankine Road, Basingstoke, Hants.

Distribution and Representation:

UNITED KINGDOM, EUROPE AND AFRICA
Chapman & Hall Ltd. (a member of Associated Book Publishers Ltd.), North Way, Andover, Hampshire.

WESTERN HEMISPHERE
Springer-Verlag New York Inc., 175 Fifth Avenue, New York, New York 10010.

AUSTRALIA, NEW ZEALAND AND FAR EAST
(EXCLUDING JAPAN)
Australia & New Zealand Book Co. Pty Ltd., P.O. Box 459, Brookvale, N.S.W. 2100.

INDIA, BANGLADESH, SRI LANKA AND BURMA
Arnold-Heinemann Publishers (India) Pvt. Ltd., AB–9, First Floor, Safjardang Enclave, New Delhi 11016.

GREECE, TURKEY, THE MIDDLE EAST (EXCLUDING ISRAEL)
Anthony Rudkin, The Old School, Speen, Aylesbury, Buckinghamshire HP17 0SL.

ALL OTHER TERRITORIES
Taylor & Francis Ltd., 10–14 Macklin Street, London, WC2B 5NF.

PREFACE

THE Wykeham Science Series is intended to bridge the gap between the syllabus work of school science and the more advanced and specialized work of a university course. I have tried to show you where the action is in real science. Meteorology and aeronomy are both modern fields that utilize classical physics. To write this book I have touched on electromagnetic theory, optics, atomic physics, mechanics, thermo-dynamics, acoustics, plasma physics and fluid mechanics.

Since the atmosphere behaves as a connected whole I would have liked to also cover meteorology. But the tropopause provides a remarkably convenient barrier demarcating meteorology from aeronomy, and also the Wykeham Science Series already has a book on meteorology: *Essentials of Meteorology* by D. H. McIntosh and A. S. Thom.

This book should be intelligible and useful to sixth formers and above, in Britain, West Africa and New Zealand; to undergraduates and above in Australia and to sophomores and above in North America. However, on first reading, some of the more difficult parts can be skipped without any loss of continuity. This is especially true of the discussion about radio wave absorption and about plasma diffusion. I especially hope that Chapter 4 will prove of value to students in colleges of technology.

It is no accident that the basic physics research most often undertaken in developing countries is either ionospheric physics or solid state physics. Both are interesting, practical, vital fields in which it is possible to make significant contributions without spending vast sums of money.

I once knew a professor of economics who believed that all of Ghana's economic problems could be solved by training more and more economists. I am not arrogant enough to claim that the training of physicists will solve all of Ghana's economic problems, but

I do believe that a corps of soundly trained scientists, engineers and technicians is a vital step on the road to development. This view is shared by the Government in Australia who have supported my work here through the Australian Development Assistance Agency.

Legon, Ghana   TOM BEER

To

Apu S Anyu

If knowledge hangs around your neck
like pearls instead of chains;
you are a lucky man.

Alan Price

LIST OF SYMBOLS

$\mathscr{A}$	area
$\mathbf{B}$	magnetic flux density
B_0, B_m	magnetic field at the equator, at the mirror point
c	speed of electromagnetic radiation in a vacuum
$c_\mathrm{v}, c_\mathrm{p}$	specific heat capacity at constant volume, at constant pressure
D_ES	Earth–Sun distance
D	coefficient of diffusion
e	an electron; the base of natural logarithms
e	electronic charge
E	energy
$\mathbf{E}$	electric field strength
f	frequency (of an electromagnetic radiation)
$f_\mathrm{B}, f_\mathrm{c}, f_0, f_\mathrm{p}$	gyro-, critical, transmitter, plasma frequency
$f_\mathrm{ob}, f_\mathrm{v}$	oblique and vertical reflection frequencies
$\mathscr{F}$	Coriolis parameter (Chapter 3)
$\mathbf{F}, \mathbf{F}_\mathrm{C}$	force, Coriolis force
g	acceleration due to gravity
G	the gravitational constant
h	the Planck constant
h_m	height of Chapman layer peak
h'	virtual height
H, H_p	scale height, plasma scale height
i	square root of minus one
I	intensity of radiation
$\mathbf{I}$	current
$\mathbf{J}$	current density
k	the Boltzmann constant
l	distance
L	loss rate
m	mass of a particle
M	molar mass (the mass of one mole, in kg)
$M_\mathrm{E}, M_\mathrm{V}, M_\mathrm{M}, M_\mathrm{J}$	mass of Earth, Venus, Mars, Jupiter
n	refractive index
N_A	the Avogadro number
N	electron density
$\mathscr{N}$	particle concentration
p	pressure

P_E, P_S	power absorbed by Earth, power emitted by Sun
q	rate of ionization production (Chapter 2)
q	electric charge
Q	total charge
r	radius of circle
r_e	lower boundary of exosphere
R	gas constant
R_E, R_M, R_J, R_V, R_S	radius of Earth, Mars, Jupiter, Venus, Sun
t	time
T	temperature
T_E, T_S, T_∞	Earth, Sun, exospheric temperature
T_e, T_i, T_n, T_p	electron, ion, neutral, plasma temperature
U	wind velocity
v, v_g	phase and group velocity
v_e	escape velocity of neutral particle
V	charged particle velocity
x, z	horizontal and vertical distance
X, Y, Z	magnetoionic symbols
α	recombination coefficient
α	pitch angle (the angle between **B** and **V**) (Chapter 6)
β	attachment-like coefficient
γ	ratio of principal specific heat capacities
ϵ_0	permittivity of a vacuum
η	dynamic viscosity
η	ionizing efficiency (Chapter 2)
θ	angle between radio wave and the magnetic field
κ	thermal conductivity
λ	wavelength
μ	kinematic viscosity
μ	real part of refractive index (Chapter 4)
μ_0	permeability of a vacuum
ν	collision frequency
ρ	density
σ	the Stefan–Boltzmann constant (Chapter 2)
σ	ionospheric conductivity (Chapter 3)
υ	absorption cross-section
ϕ	angle between radio wave and the ionosphere
Φ	phase angle
ϕ	latitude (Chapter 3)
χ	solar zenith angle
χ	imaginary part of refractive index (Chapter 4)
ω	angular frequency
ω_p	angular plasma frequency

Ω Faraday rotation angle

Ω_E angular velocity of the Earth

Constants

$$c = 3{\cdot}0 \times 10^8 \text{ m s}^{-1}$$
$$D_{ES} = 1{\cdot}5 \times 10^8 \text{ km}$$
$$e = -1{\cdot}6 \times 10^{-19} \text{ C}$$
$$g = 9{\cdot}8 \text{ m s}^{-1}$$
$$G = 6{\cdot}67 \times 10^{-11} \text{ N m}^2 \text{ kg}^{-2}$$
$$h = 6{\cdot}63 \times 10^{-34} \text{ J s}$$
$$k = 1{\cdot}38 \times 10^{-23} \text{ J K}^{-1}$$
$$m_e = 9{\cdot}1 \times 10^{-31} \text{ kg}$$
$$M_E = 5{\cdot}98 \times 10^{24} \text{ kg}$$
$$N_A = 6{\cdot}02 \times 10^{23} \text{ mol}^{-1}$$
$$R = 8{\cdot}31 \text{ J mol}^{-1} \text{ K}^{-1}$$
$$R_E = 6{\cdot}37 \times 10^3 \text{ km}$$
$$R_S = 7{\cdot}0 \times 10^5 \text{ km}$$
$$T_S = 5750 \text{ K}$$
$$\epsilon_0 = 8{\cdot}854 \times 10^{-12} \text{ F m}^{-1}$$
$$\mu_0 = 4\pi \times 10^{-7} \text{ H m}^{-1}$$
$$\sigma = 5{\cdot}67 \times 10^{-8} \text{ J m}^{-2} \text{ K}^{-4} \text{ s}^{-1}$$
$$\Omega_E = 7{\cdot}29 \times 10^{-5} \text{ rad s}^{-1}$$

ACKNOWLEDGMENTS

I WISH to thank the following journals, publishers, organizations and individuals for their permission to reproduce previously published material or for providing illustrations.

Fig. 1.3   From Prof. G. S. Kent, 1970, *Reviews of Geophysics and Space Physics*, **75**, 241, copyright by the American Geophysical Union.

Fig. 1.5   Dr. J. W. King and Dr. H. Rishbeth.

Figs. 1.6 and 3.9   Dr. H. Rishbeth.

Fig. 2.10   These diagrams first appeared in the *New Scientist*, London.

Figs. 3.11, 5.7 and 6.4   From *Sun, Earth and Radio* by J. A. Ratcliffe. Published by Weidenfeld and Nicolson.

Fig. 4.13   Photo by the United States Information Service.

Figs. 5.2 and 5.4   Reproduced with the permission of the editor of the *Journal of Atmospheric and Terrestrial Physics*. Published by Pergamon Press.

Fig. 5.3   Dr. J. Thomas and Dr. H. Rishbeth.

Fig. 6.1   From Dr. Luigi G. Jacchia, CIRA 1965, page 295. Published by North Holland Publishing Company, P.O. Box 103, Amsterdam.

Figs. 6.6, 6.10 and 6.11   From *An Introduction to the Ionosphere and Magnetosphere* by J. A. Ratcliffe. Published by Cambridge University Press.

Fig. 6.8   These auroral photographs are by Gustav Lamprecht, P.O. Box 80825, College, Alaska.

CONTENTS

CHAPTER 1

introduction

1.1. *The atmosphere*

FOUR thousand million years ago, the Earth had an atmosphere composed primarily of hydrogen, methane, water vapour and ammonia. It was in this atmosphere that the amino acids which are the building blocks of life were formed. Because of the rapid rotation of the young planet Earth this primitive atmosphere escaped, to be gradually replaced by the present atmosphere which is composed of nitrogen, oxygen and carbon dioxide along with various other minor constituents. The proportion of each constituent in the atmosphere varies with altitude. For example, hydrogen and helium are the dominant species at the outer extremities of the atmosphere. This atmosphere governs our whole life.

This book will be concerned with the Earth's upper atmosphere at altitudes greater than 20 km. Below this height lies the lower atmosphere which influences the Earth's weather. The study of the lower atmosphere is known as meteorology; the study of the upper atmosphere is called aeronomy, which refers to the science of that part of the upper atmosphere where dissociation and ionization are important. Often meteorology and aeronomy overlap, because the atmosphere acts as a whole and the events that occur at any particular part of it are influenced by the processes occurring elsewhere.

Aeronomers are forward-looking people and talk of the direction towards which a wind is blowing whereas meteorologists look backward and refer to the direction from which a wind has come! The aeronomer's eastward wind becomes the meteorologist's westerly wind.

The upper atmosphere can be a site of great beauty. In the polar regions there are often spectacular displays of the northern lights and the southern lights, and all over the world, meteors leave their glowing trails. It is also of great practical use. Modern telecommunications utilize the radio-wave reflecting properties of one part of the upper atmosphere called the ionosphere. The upper atmosphere is also of great scientific interest, for its chemistry, its physics and its dynamics are still imperfectly understood.

From 50 km upwards, the atmosphere is ionized. This means that there exist free ions, and free electrons which have escaped from

1

the molecules that comprise the atmosphere; hence the name ionosphere. A mixture of ions, electrons and neutral (un-ionized) particles is called a plasma, and plasmas have been described as the fourth state of matter. On Earth the other three states predominate—the solids, the liquids and the gases. But over 99% of the universe is plasma—for example, the Sun is a hot dense gaseous plasma. Most important to the aeronomer, the ionosphere is a cold gaseous plasma composed of equal numbers of electrons and positive ions. (Though the ionosphere can reach temperatures as high as 2000 K this is cold when compared to the Sun.) The plasma physicist can use the Earth's upper atmosphere as a gigantic laboratory to study the behaviour of a large-scale plasma being acted upon by the Earth's magnetic field.

The behaviour of the whole atmosphere is governed by the Sun. The absorption of solar radiation is responsible for nearly everything that goes on in the Earth's atmosphere. The electrons which comprise the ionosphere each initially absorbed a quantum of energy from the incoming solar radiation and then jumped out of the molecule or atom holding them. Furthermore, the temperature of the atmosphere is determined by the ability of the atmospheric gases to absorb radiation energy. Every atom or molecule can absorb radiation at certain characteristic wavelengths. A photon of sufficient energy can excite or ionize a particle, which then collides with an unexcited or un-ionized particle and in the process loses its extra energy by giving it up to the other particle in the form of kinetic energy. An increase in the average kinetic energy of the particles corresponds to an increase in temperature. We would thus expect the atmosphere to have higher temperatures where there are concentrations of efficient absorbers of the radiation passing through it.

The Earth's surface temperature is determined by a balance between the incoming solar radiation, which is characteristic of a black body at 6000 K, and the outgoing terrestrial radiation which is characteristic of a grey body at 290 K. The natural radiation that goes out from the surface of the earth is almost entirely in the infrared part of the electromagnetic spectrum with a maximum at about $10 \mu m$. On the other hand, the radiant energy coming from the Sun is rich in ultraviolet as well as visible light, with a maximum at about 600 nm.

The absorption of radiation determines the temperature structure of the atmosphere (fig. 1.1). In the lowest 15 km of the atmosphere, the re-radiated infrared part of the spectrum is absorbed by water vapour and carbon dioxide. Since there is a gradual decrease in the amount of water vapour and carbon dioxide in the air as we ascend, the temperature in the lowest part of the atmosphere, which is known as the troposphere, decreases with altitude. The troposphere terminates at the tropopause where a local minimum temperature is

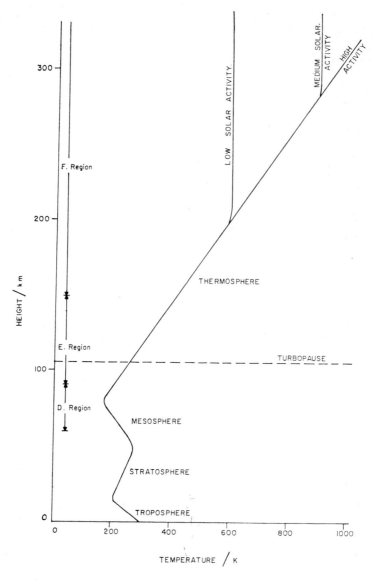

Fig. 1.1.   Atmospheric temperature structure and nomenclature.

reached, usually at heights in the range 7–17 km, depending on the latitude and season. The tropopause is a natural 'lid' on the lower atmosphere. Above it lies the upper atmosphere.

The temperature structure of the upper atmosphere is completely determined by each region's ability to absorb the incoming solar radiation. Between 35 and 70 km there is a trace of ozone, O_3, in the atmosphere. Although it is a very minor constituent, contributing only a few millionths of the total ground-level pressure, ozone is extraordinarily efficient in absorbing the ultraviolet radiation. Because of the ozone, the temperature above the tropopause starts to increase with height, reaching a maximum at the stratopause at about 45–55 km. This region of temperature inversion, or positive temperature gradient is known as the stratosphere. The temperature then declines in the mesosphere to a minimum at the mesopause near 80–85 km. Ozone cannot exist in the mesosphere or above. The mesopause is the coldest level in the entire atmosphere.

The temperature begins to rise again above the mesopause and this region is known as the thermosphere. At these heights a significant part of the air is composed of atomic oxygen, O, and the thermosphere exists because molecular oxygen is an efficient absorber of very short wavelength ultraviolet radiation which converts the molecular oxygen into atomic oxygen. In the thermosphere the neutral gas temperature increases up to an altitude of 200 km and then remains constant vertically to heights exceeding 1000 km. This isothermal behaviour of the upper thermosphere arises because its thermal conductivity is so high that most of the energy absorbed by the gas is conducted downwards.

The ozone and molecular oxygen present at these levels are just as vital to life as the air that we breathe. They absorb the lethal ultraviolet and short wavelength radiation and so help to make life possible on the earth's surface.

The limiting thermospheric temperature is determined by the incoming ultraviolet radiation. Solar heat input depends mainly on the angle of incidence of the Sun's rays and this produces seasonal, daily and latitudinal differences in temperature. However there are also fluctuations in heat input that vary periodically over a solar sunspot cycle. During periods of very high solar activity the Sun emits much more ultraviolet radiation and the thermosphere temperature can reach 2200 K. At solar minimum no part of the atmosphere reaches a higher temperature than 750 K.

In the thermosphere the distribution of the gases is controlled by diffusion. Because of this, a transition from mainly atomic oxygen ions to primarily helium ions takes place at about 1000 km, and from helium ions to the lighter hydrogen ions at heights of the order of 3000 km. However, both the hydrogen and helium can attain

4

sufficient velocity to escape the Earth's gravitational field, so that there must be some source of hydrogen and helium in the atmosphere producing these elements. If there were no production of the light elements, we should have lost all of the Earth's original hydrogen and helium by now. Helium is an end product of radioactive processes in rocks, and volcanoes eject it into the atmosphere in a concentration of 5 parts of helium to a million parts of air (5 p.p.m.). Hydrogen is produced higher in the atmosphere by ultraviolet radiation breaking water vapour into hydrogen and oxygen. There are 0·5 p.p.m. of molecular hydrogen in the atmosphere from ground level to 100 km.

The very short wavelength components of the solar radiation ionize the neutral particles so that a region of free electrons, ions and neutral particles exists in the upper atmosphere. This region is known as the ionosphere and it consists of three main regions. The D region at heights of 60 to 90 km, the E region from 90 to 150 km and the F region from 150 km to the top of the atmosphere. In addition to the regular regions of the ionosphere there are occasionally regions of a transient or irregular nature, and there are also a large number of different types of irregularity. Remembering that temperature is proportional to the average kinetic energy of the particles concerned, at a given site in the D and E regions the temperatures of all the atmospheric constituents are equal. This is no longer true of the F region, in which the electron temperature exceeds the ion temperature, which in turn exceeds the neutral gas temperature. The reason for this is discussed in Chapter 5.

So far we have mentioned two important parameters that determine the state of the upper atmosphere—the neutral gas temperature, T, which is measured in kelvins and the degree of ionization which is measured by the number of electrons in a cubic metre and which will be represented by the symbol N. There are other significant parameters as well, the most important being the pressure p (Pa) the density ρ (kg m^{-3}) and the molar mass M (kg mol^{-1}).* The atmospheric water vapour content which is an important quantity in the troposphere is generally negligible in the upper atmosphere. All the parameters are not independent however. The air acts very much like an ideal gas, and the equation of state for an ideal gas connects the pressure, density, temperature and molar mass

$$p = \rho R T / M \qquad (1.1)$$

where the gas constant $R = 8 \cdot 31$ J mol^{-1} K^{-1}.

Even though there are both temporal and spatial variations in these parameters, it has been possible to tabulate average values for these

* Here M stands for the average mass of a mole measured in kilograms. The 'molecular weight', or relative molecular mass, is $0 \cdot 012 \, M/M_0$, where M_0 is the mass of one mole of ^{12}C atoms.

quantities. These tables are known as standard atmospheres, and a number of them exist. The two most widely used in aeronomy are the United States Standard Atmosphere of 1962 (published by the U.S. Government Printing Office) and the COSPAR International Reference Atmosphere of 1972—usually abbreviated to CIRA 1972 (published by Akademie-Verlag of Berlin).

Table 1.1 is an extract from a standard atmosphere which gives mean values of the atmospheric parameters. The density and pressure both decrease sharply as the height increases. In fact density and pressure are related by

$$\mathrm{d}p/\mathrm{d}z = -\rho g \qquad (1.2)$$

which is known as the hydrostatic equation.

Let us eliminate the density from equations (1.1) and (1.2) by using the ideal gas equation. This gives

$$\frac{\mathrm{d}p}{\mathrm{d}z} = -\frac{Mg}{RT}p \qquad (1.3)$$

so that if the vertical variation of T, M and g are known, then the vertical variation of pressure may be found by integration. But if M, g, R, T are all supposed constant then

$$p = p_0 \exp\left(-\frac{Mg}{RT}z\right)$$

The scale height H is defined as

$$H = RT/Mg$$

Since the temperature T varies with altitude so will H. The scale height is the height in which the pressure distribution would be reduced to $0\cdot368$ ($=1/e$) of its original value p_0. The value of H ranges from about 7 km in the troposphere to a minimum of 5 km at the mesopause at an altitude of 80–90 km. It then rises in the thermosphere, eventually reaching a value of around 100 km. Even when the temperature has reached its isothermal value, H continues to increase slowly as M and g both decrease.

The last column in Table 1.1 gives values for the gas concentration, in terms of the number of atmospheric particles per cubic metre ($\mathcal{N}$). Once again this quantity is not independent, but is related to the density by

$$\rho = \frac{M\mathcal{N}}{N_A}$$

where N_A is the Avogadro constant, $6\cdot02 \times 10^{23}$ mol^{-1}. Below 100 km the gas concentration is made up of 78% molecular nitrogen (N_2), 21% molecular oxygen (O_2) and various other minor constituents

6

Table 1.1. Extract from a standard atmosphere. $8\cdot81(-5)$ represents $8\cdot81 \times 10^{-5}$.

Height $\dfrac{z}{\text{km}}$	Gas temperature $\dfrac{T}{\text{K}}$	Scale height $\dfrac{H}{\text{km}}$	Molar mass $\dfrac{M}{\text{kg mol}^{-1}}$	Pressure $\dfrac{p}{\text{Pa}}$	Density $\dfrac{\rho}{\text{kg m}^{-3}}$	Neutral gas concentration $\dfrac{\mathcal{N}}{\text{m}^{-3}}$	
30	230	6·81	2·896(−2)	1·20(3)	1·82(−2)	3·78(23)	} Stratosphere
40	251	7·44	2·896(−2)	2·94(2)	4·09(−3)	8·51(22)	
50	271	8·07	2·896(−2)	8·10(1)	1·04(−3)	2·16(22)	Stratopause
60	243	7·27	2·896(−2)	2·20(1)	3·14(−4)	6·54(21)	} Mesosphere
70	217	6·49	2·896(−2)	5·12	8·23(−5)	1·71(21)	
80	186	5·59	2·896(−2)	9·75(−1)	1·83(−5)	3·80(20)	Mesopause
100	208	6·44	2·830(−2)	3·10(−2)	5·06(−7)	1·08(19)	
120	355	11·58	2·701(−2)	2·73(−3)	2·50(−8)	5·57(17)	
140	573	19·74	2·575(−2)	7·50(−4)	4·05(−9)	9·50(16)	
160	721	26·15	2·461(−2)	3·13(−4)	1·28(−9)	3·15(16)	
180	840	32·00	2·356(−2)	1·57(−4)	5·29(−10)	1·36(16)	
200	934	37·37	2·258(−2)	8·81(−5)	2·56(−10)	6·88(15)	Thermosphere
250	1078	48·27	2·048(−2)	2·74(−5)	6·26(−11)	1·86(15)	
300	1144	56·42	1·887(−2)	1·06(−5)	2·10(−11)	6·75(14)	
400	1184	67·4	1·683(−2)	2·11(−6)	3·61(−12)	1·29(14)	
500	1192	75·6	1·556(−2)	5·19(−7)	8·15(−13)	3·16(13)	
600	1194	86·3	1·406(−2)	1·50(−7)	2·12(−13)	9·07(12)	

7

However, at 108 km altitude there lies the turbopause, above which the air is no longer turbulent. The percentage of each constituent stays the same below the turbopause because turbulent mixing is always taking place so that none of the individual constituents can settle down. This is a good thing because it is this turbulent mixing that disperses the smoke from factory chimneys and motor cars; without it each factory chimney would have its base covered in its own smoke. Since the percentage of each constituent stays the same, the mean molecular mass of the atmosphere below 100 km also stays constant.

The situation above the turbopause is quite different. No turbulent mixing is going on here, so each gas tries to settle. The density of each gas above the turbopause decreases exponentially, with the heavier gases being concentrated closer to the bottom of the region of non-turbulent flow. This causes the percentage of N_2 and O_2 to decrease quickly as one rises above 100 km. From 150 km to 600 km the chief atmospheric constituent is atomic oxygen, O, and above 600 km hydrogen and helium predominate. Thus above 100 km there is a steady decline in the mean molecular mass of the atmosphere. The region of the upper atmosphere in which hydrogen and helium predominate is called the exosphere.

1.2. *Measuring the properties of the atmosphere*

Turbulent mixing in the atmosphere takes place by convection. In general convective motions, as in the troposphere, will tend to set up an equilibrium, called adiabatic equilibrium, in which air packets can move up or down without losing or gaining heat. It can be shown mathematically, by using the adiabatic equation of state for a gas along with the hydrostatic equation (1.2), that there will be a natural ceiling to a purely adiabatic atmosphere at a height of about 28 km. Before World War I it was generally believed that this height did indeed represent the limit to the Earth's atmosphere.

During World War I it was observed that people at a certain distance from a large explosion would fail to hear it, though other people even further away could hear it quite clearly. (A notable case was the disastrous explosion of a munitions factory at Silvertown in 1917.) This phenomenon came to be referred to as anomalous sound propagation.

Though anomalous sound propagation had been identified and partly explained as early as 1904, it was not till after the war that it was pointed out that it was caused by a region above the troposphere in which the temperature increases with height. Temperature gradients, as well as wind gradients, distort the wave-fronts and so refract sound waves. Anomalous sound propagation occurred both downwind and upwind so that it must have been occasioned by a temperature inversion in the upper atmosphere (i.e. change to a regime in which temperature increases with height) as in fig. 1.2. The sound wave moving parallel to the ground is moving through denser air and will be absorbed more than the sound wave that is reflected at the less dense stratosphere.

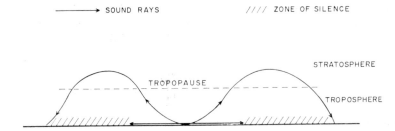

———→ SOUND RAYS   //// ZONE OF SILENCE

Fig. 1.2. Anomalous sound propagation. Only one representative sound ray is shown.

Surprisingly, deductions as to the mesospheric and thermospheric temperatures followed quickly from the study of the heights at which meteors disappeared. It had long been suspected that meteors were lumps of rock being heated to the point of glowing by air friction. On the other hand, this idea has not always met with universal acclaim. Galileo (1564–1642) scornfully pointed out that if air resistance could heat things then we should be able to cook an egg by tying it to a piece of string and twirling rapidly. But just over fifty years ago F. A. Lindemann and G. M. B. Dobson were able to describe the process (and show, incidentally, that these were *very small* solid particles burning away, rather than lumps of hot rock). It turns out that a knowledge of the meteor's velocity, density, radius, thermal conductivity and specific heat capacity enable one to determine the atmospheric density at the height of appearance and at the height of disappearance. These two values are independent and it was found that the only way that the readings would make sense was to assume a high stratospheric temperature which drops to a minimum at about 80 km and rises again above this height.

All of these predictions became directly verifiable after the Second World War when balloons were developed that could attain heights of 50 km, and rockets that could be sent even higher were built. The balloons used for routine atmospheric soundings carry an instrument package known as a radio-sonde. This consists of sensors which directly transmit values of the pressure, temperature and humidity to a ground-based radio receiver. Meanwhile, the receiver is also tracking the balloon to obtain information about the direction and strength of the wind.

Rockets rise too quickly to allow direct readings to be taken of the neutral atmosphere, though they can carry apparatus to measure the properties of the charged particles. One useful instrument is known as a Langmuir probe and it is used to measure the electron concentration and the electron temperature.

A very useful method of determining winds and temperatures in the upper stratosphere and mesosphere is to fire a series of grenades from an ascending rocket. The exact time and location of each explosion is known and the exact time and angle of arrival of the sound waves can be measured, and the winds and temperatures calculated. Measurements of the rate of fall of spheres released from the rocket can provide density measurements provided that the atmosphere is not too tenuous. Another method of measuring the density at these heights is to shine a searchlight beam, or more recently a laser beam, vertically upwards from the ground. A photo-sensitive detector then scans the searchlight beam to determine the intensity of the scattered light as a function of altitude, which can be related to the density of the air molecules.

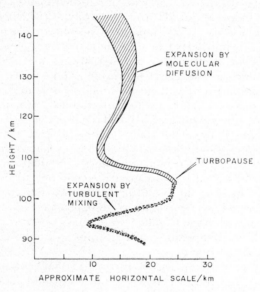

Fig. 1.3. A luminous trail, a few minutes after formation.

Rockets are also used to lay down a luminous trail behind them, so that the wind can be found by measuring the deformation of the trail. It was this method that led to the discovery of the turbopause since the deformation above and below the turbopause is strikingly different (fig. 1.3).

10

It becomes very difficult to establish the atmospheric properties above 200 km. Since 1957 it has been possible to track satellites, and to measure the variations in a satellite's time of revolution around the Earth that are caused by the retarding force of air friction. The rate of change of the period of a satellite is proportional to the gas density and to the height of the orbit, so that ρ can easily be obtained. The hydrostatic equation and the ideal gas equation can then give the neutral gas temperature.

Satellites offer excellent observing platforms for meteorologists since they can easily photograph large areas of the globe, and provide early warnings of hurricanes. The same satellites can also use a radiometer to measure the infrared radiation emitted from the surface of the Earth, or from cloud tops, and calculate the emitting temperatures. By observing CO_2 emissions at 15 μm with sophisticated radiometers it is possible to obtain a profile of the variation of temperature with altitude up to 50 km.

Satellites orbit at heights above 200 km, at which the atmosphere is ionized. They can be used to make direct measurements in these regions, but it is a rather difficult task. For continuous readings it is easier and cheaper to examine the ionosphere with radio waves and to make deductions about the upper atmosphere from these observations.

1.3. The ionosphere

In 1901 G. Marconi (1874–1937) astonished the world by successfully transmitting radio signals across the Atlantic. The controversy over why this occurred was settled in 1925, when E. V. Appleton and M. A. F. Barnett in England and G. Breit and M. A. Tuve in America experimentally verified the existence of a conducting layer above the Earth's surface that could reflect radio signals. This conducting layer is composed of ions and electrons, and reflection is due to the interaction of the electrons with the electromagnetic fields of the radio wave. For verification of the ionosphere's existence, and for the many fundamental experiments that he did in upper atmosphere physics, Appleton (1892–1965) was awarded the 1947 Nobel prize in physics.

The most popular method of examining the ionosphere is by a sweep frequency sounder known as an ionosonde. This is a radio transmitter that transmits a signal vertically whose frequency continuously varies from 0·5 MHz to 10 MHz. The time delay of the reflected signal as the frequency changes is displayed on a picture which is called an ionogram. If we know the time it took for the signal to return and if we assume that the signal travelled at the speed of light $(3\cdot0 \times 10^8$ m s$^{-1})$ then we can find the height at which reflection occurred. In fact the radio wave takes an appreciable amount of time

11

to turn around during reflection, so that the height determined by this method is known as the virtual height. An idealized ionogram is shown in fig. 1.4.

Radio waves will be reflected provided that their frequency f is below a critical frequency f_c where

$$f_c{}^2 = Ne^2/(4\pi^2\epsilon_0 m_e)$$

where

N = number of electrons per cubic metre (called the electron density),

e/m_e = specific charge of the electrons,

ϵ_0 = permittivity of a vacuum.

So that we may write, after substituting numerical values

$$f_c = \sqrt{(80 \cdot 6 N)} \approx 9 N^{1/2} \text{ Hz} \qquad (1.4)$$

If there is a local peak in the ionization density, as there is at the points marked f_{cE} and f_{cF2}, then the ionogram trace is broken. If there is a ' ledge ' (a mathematician would call it a point of inflexion) then the trace is continuous as at f_{cF1}.

The process of converting an ionogram into a graph of electron density as a function of altitude is known as ionogram reduction. Unfortunately, the results obtained are not unique. There are a number of possible electron density profiles that could fit fig. 1.4.

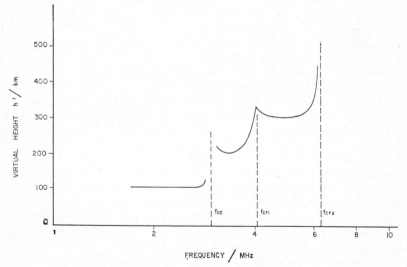

Fig. 1.4. Idealized daytime ionogram.

12

However, on the basis of many ionosonde observations the presence of an E region peak, a ledge in the F region (known as the F1 ledge) during daytime and an F region peak (the F2 peak) were well established. Later on, the D region was found below the E region, with an electron density two orders of magnitude smaller than the E region's.

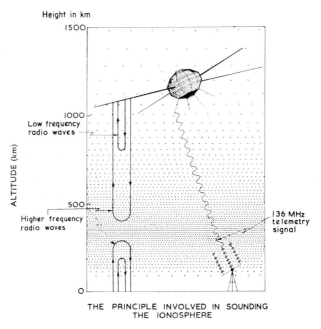

THE PRINCIPLE INVOLVED IN SOUNDING
THE IONOSPHERE

Fig. 1.5. Topside and bottomside ionospheric sounding. The density of dots indicates the electron density. Information obtained by the satellite has to be sent to the ground by very high frequency signals which are not reflected by the ionosphere.

A ground-based ionogram gives absolutely no information on the electron density structure above the F region peak. Since the sixties, ionograms of this region have been obtained from topside soundings carried out by ionosonde-carrying satellites. The principle involved in sounding the ionosphere from above and below is shown in fig. 1.5. The density of dots roughly indicates the electron density, greatest at around 300 km. The higher the frequency of the probing wave, the deeper it penetrates into the ionosphere before being returned. Information obtained by the satellite has to be sent to the ground by radio signals at a very high frequency, such as 136 MHz which easily penetrates the ionosphere. Yet this telemetry signal can also be used to study the ionosphere. We in Ghana have been observing

13

the 136 MHz telemetry signal from the satellite ATS 3 and we find that it is unintelligible at night. This is caused by an effect, to be discussed in Section 5.5, called spread F.

Direct confirmation of the ionospheric structure deduced from ionograms was obtained when rockets were shot through the ionosphere carrying Langmuir probes. We can imagine how a Langmuir probe works by thinking of a battery, an ammeter and a parallel plate capacitor made of two plates of equal cross-sectional area $\mathscr{A}$. The three are connected in series and when there are electrons between the capacitor plates they are attracted to the positive plate. This causes a current to flow. The current read on the ammeter, $\mathbf{I}$, is given by

$$\mathbf{I} = Ne\mathscr{A}V$$

where V, the drift speed of the electrons can be found by knowing (or assuming) the neutral gas density and the battery voltage. Since e, the electronic charge, and $\mathscr{A}$ are known the electron density can be found.

The overall structure of the ionosphere is depicted in fig. 1.6. We shall discuss the detailed structure of each region in Chapter 5.

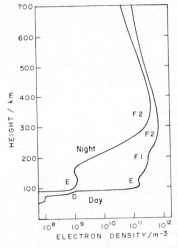

Fig. 1.6. Typical electron density profiles.

1.4. The Earth's magnetic field

By the time we reach heights of 500 km almost all the atmosphere is ionized. A charged particle's motion is strongly controlled by the electric and magnetic fields surrounding it, so that a knowledge of

14

the structure of the Earth's magnetic field is essential to the understanding of ionospheric motions.

Close to the surface of the Earth, the Earth's magnetic field is similar to that of a simple bar magnet. This is known as a dipole field. Before the International Geophysical Year (IGY) in 1957–8, it was believed that the Earth's dipole field continued to extend outwards into space without changing its shape. After the intensive rocket and satellite observations during the IGY, it was gradually realized that as one ascends, the magnetic field begins to look less and less like that of a dipole. It is flattened on the sunny side and elongated on the night side (fig. 1.7).

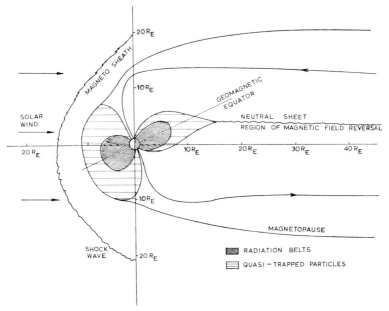

Fig. 1.7. The magnetosphere. The unit for the axes is the Earth's radius, $6\cdot37 \times 10^6$ m.

The distortion of the Earth's magnetic field arises from its interaction with the solar wind. The solar wind is caused by the outer atmosphere of the Sun, the corona, which is a gas with a temperature of about 2×10^6 K. It is so hot that it simply 'expands outwards into space'. Although the Sun has a strong gravitational field, the two million degrees temperature of the gas denotes enough kinetic energy to make the particles stream outward. They stream outward all the time and in all directions from the Sun.

15

The solar wind is composed almost completely of hydrogen. But at these high temperatures the hydrogen is ionized, so that the solar wind is a plasma of hydrogen ions (protons) and electrons travelling at speeds that range from $300 \, \text{km s}^{-1}$ to $1000 \, \text{km s}^{-1}$, depending on the solar activity.

Internal motions in the Sun generate magnetic fields. The solar wind, being a stream of charged particles, is responsible for extending the magnetic field of the Sun. In effect, it carries the field with it and ' stretches the lines of force from the Sun as if they were infinitely extensible rubber bands, though of course the magnetic fields now are those associated with the charged particles moving as a stream '. Interplanetary space is full of weak magnetic fields originating in this way from the Sun. While the particles move outward in a radial direction, however, the Sun is rotating, completing one revolution in about 27 days. The result is the so-called ' garden hose ' effect— the field lines assuming the spiral form that a rotating jet of water from a garden hose is seen to have. The solar wind drags the magnetic field lines radially outward to great distances. But since the individual lines are firmly rooted in the rotating Sun, they are wound into a spiral form (fig. 1.8).

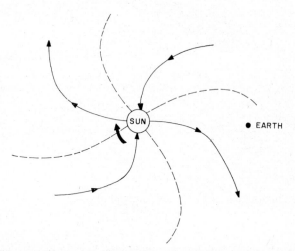

Fig. 1.8. The ' garden hose ' effect. The interplanetary magnetic field points either towards or away from the Sun, with the dashed lines marking the boundaries between the two orientations. As the Sun rotates the field at the Earth changes direction every 27 days.

The 1970 Nobel prize in physics was awarded to the Swedish physicist Hannes Alfvén (born 1908) for his discovery that magnetic field lines can propagate a transverse oscillation now known as an

Alfvén wave. The velocity of an Alfvén wave is analogous to the velocity of sound in air. An object moving faster than the speed of sound in air is supersonic and sets up a shock front. A magnetic field moving faster than the velocity of Alfvén waves is superalfvénic and also sets up a shock front. The solar wind is 'superalfvénic' and when the interplanetary magnetic fields that are imbedded in it hit the magnetic field of the Earth they distort it, but do not normally penetrate it. The distortion is depicted in fig. 1.7 and we can see that the Earth's magnetic field is an enclosed tear-shaped cavity inside the solar wind. This enclosed region is known as the magnetosphere of the Earth.

Since the interplanetary magnetic fields are superalfvénic, a shock front develops at their boundary with the Earth's magnetic field. In the vicinity of this shock front the magnetic fields are disturbed and the plasma is turbulent; this is the region called the magnetosheath. Behind the magnetosheath the Earth's magnetic field firmly establishes itself, the magnetopause marking the furthest limit of the Earth's magnetic field.

The charged particles comprising the Earth's exosphere will not be able to escape from the magnetosphere so that the magnetopause acts as an effective limit to the Earth's atmosphere. However, within this boundary there are certain regions where charged particles are trapped (fig. 1.7). Charged particles tend to move along magnetic field lines because motion at right angles to the lines causes a force which tends to bring the particle back to the line. Only those areas where both ends of the magnetic field touch the Earth can trap particles. In the outer trapping regions the particles stand an equal chance of diffusing out of the trapping region, or of diffusing further into it—these particles are only quasi-trapped. There are certain areas within the trapping regions of the magnetosphere where the concentration of trapped particles is very high. These areas are known as the Van Allen radiation belts.

The motion of charged particles in the ionosphere and magnetosphere is strongly controlled by the electric and magnetic fields present in these regions. The next section will review the essentials of the motion of charged particles under electromagnetic forces.

1.5. *The motion of charged particles*

We have seen that the limit of the Earth's atmosphere is determined by the limit of the Earth's magnetic field. This occurs because charged particles in the magnetosphere are able to move only along magnetic field lines, in just the same way that a pearl in a necklace can only slide along the thread.

When you inject a charged particle into a magnetic field, it experiences a force whose magnitude, $F = qV_{\perp}B$, is determined by the charge, the magnetic flux density and its velocity perpendicular to the field. The direction of this force is normal to both the field and to the perpendicular component of velocity so that the particle describes a circle. If the particle has a velocity component $V_{\parallel}$ parallel to the magnetic field, then it tends also to move in the direction of the field with velocity $V_{\parallel}$, describing a helix (fig. 1.9 (a)).

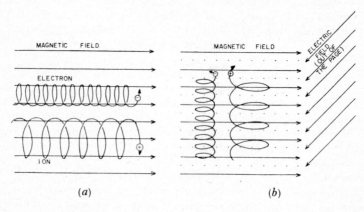

(a) (b)

Fig. 1.9. (a) Charged particles in a magnetic field will spiral around the magnetic field lines. (b) When an electric field is introduced at right angles to the magnetic field then the particles drift in a direction at right angles to both fields.

The number of revolutions described by the charged particle in a second is called the gyrofrequency, since the particle is gyrating in circles about the magnetic field line. The gyrofrequency f_B is independent of the velocity, being given by

$$f_B = qB/2\pi m$$

where m is the mass of the particle. This is simply derived by noting that since the magnetic force deflecting the particle keeps it moving in a circle, it must be the centripetal force for the motion, so that if the circle has a radius r then

$$\frac{mV_{\perp}^{2}}{r} = m\omega_B^2 r = qV_{\perp}B$$

where

$$V_{\perp} = r\omega_B = r2\pi f_B$$

The Earth's magnetic field is about 0.5×10^{-4} T at ionospheric heights so that the electron gyrofrequency in the ionosphere is 1.4 MHz and the ion gyrofrequency is below 760 Hz, which is the gyrofrequency of H^+.

18

We should notice that the electron gyrofrequency falls in the radio-frequency range in which ionosondes normally operate. This is an important point because it means that a real ionogram is not going to be as simple as the one shown in fig. 1.4. There is an interaction between the radio wave, the magnetic field, and the electron so that on a real ionosonde one sees two slightly different traces. The effects of the magnetic field is to split the ionosonde trace in two.

An electric field accelerates a positive ion in the direction of the field and an electron in the direction opposite to the field. If an electric and magnetic field both act on a charged particle, then the component of the electric field that is *parallel to the magnetic field* accelerates the charged particle along the magnetic line of force.

The component of the electric field *perpendicular to the magnetic field* produces a more complicated motion. In crossed electric and magnetic fields a charged particle drifts in a direction perpendicular to both fields, with both electrons and ions drifting in the same direction. This can be explained in outline as follows. The electric field always exerts a force* $\mathbf{F} = q\mathbf{E}$ on the particles. If q is positive (ions), then $\mathbf{F}$ and $\mathbf{E}$ are parallel; if q is negative (electrons), they are antiparallel. From this it appears that the electric field which gives a positive ion a velocity-component $+V_{\perp}$ at right angles to $\mathbf{B}$ will give an electron a velocity-component $-V_{\perp}'$ in the opposite direction. So we get for the '$qV_{\perp}$' products $(+q \times +V_{\perp})$ for the positive ion and $(-q \times -V_{\perp}')$ for the electron—*both* positive and so both in the same direction for both kinds of particle.

The product '$qV_{\perp}$' is always going to have the same sign so that the drift force, $qV_{\perp}B$, will always be in the same direction for both particles. Since this direction is perpendicular to both $V_{\perp}$ and $\mathbf{B}$, the charged particles will drift perpendicular to both $\mathbf{E}$ and $\mathbf{B}$ (fig. 1.9 (b)). It is called an '$\mathbf{E} \times \mathbf{B}$ drift' and the magnitude of the drift velocity is E/B.

In the magnetosphere the particle motions are completely controlled by the electric and magnetic fields that are there. Thus, if observations of magnetospheric charged particles indicate that they are not moving wholly in a direction parallel to the magnetic field then, by measuring their velocities, the direction and magnitude of the magnetospheric electric fields can be determined.

Within a perfect electrical conductor, the electric field strength must be zero. Since the ionosphere is basically a good conductor we would expect the electric fields in the upper atmosphere to be small. This is indeed the case. The observed magnitudes of the

* I am using bold letters, e.g. $\mathbf{F}$, $\mathbf{E}$, $\mathbf{B}$ to denote a vector—a quantity with both magnitude and direction. If I am only talking about the magnitude of the quantity I use a normal F, E, B, etc.

ionospheric and magnetospheric electric fields range from 1 to 10 mV m^{-1}.

In the D and E regions of the ionosphere the picture is even more complicated. In these regions of the ionosphere, the charged particles will collide with the neutral molecules of the air. The collision frequency is the number of collisions per second that a charged particle makes with the neutral particles; see Table 1.2. The collision frequency is going to depend primarily on the number of neutral particles there are around obstructing the motion of the charged particles. Since the number of neutral particles decreases exponentially with height, so also does each collision frequency, and by F region altitudes the collisions with neutrals are not important in the electrodynamic motions. At F region heights it is the collisions between the charged species, the electron–ion collisions that will dominate.

Height	100 km	200 km	300 km
ion—neutral ν_{in}	5800 s^{-1}	4·1 s^{-1}	0·5 s^{-1}
electron—neutral ν_{en}	92 000 s^{-1}	130 s^{-1}	15 s^{-1}
electron—ion ν_{ei}	2000 s^{-1}	500 s^{-1}	1000 s^{-1}

Table 1.2.   Collision frequencies.

In the D region the gyrofrequency is about equal to the collision frequency, and the effect of the magnetic field on the particles is reduced (see fig. 1.10). The electrons and positive ions follow the direction of any electric field they encounter—as they would in the absence of a magnetic field. Since electrons and positive ions have opposite charge, their velocity components in the direction of the electric field are opposite to each other, which is another way of saying that each contributes to carrying an electric current.

Electrons gyrate many times more around magnetic field lines before hitting neutral atoms or molecules because the mass of an electron is far less than the mass of a positive ion. Hence there is a range of altitudes, comprising the E region, where the electrons are still drifting as they would in free space in the absence of collisions, whereas the ions are already strongly affected by collisions with the neutral molecules. The resulting gain of ion mobility in the direction of the transverse electric field gives rise to a current, known as the

Pedersen current. At the same time, the reduction of the drift of the ions at right angles to the electric field causes another electric current—the Hall current. In fig. 1.10 the magnetic field is directed up out of the page, so that if there were no collisions the $\mathbf{E} \times \mathbf{B}$ drift would be to the right. At lower altitudes (fig. 1.10 (*b*)) an ion cannot complete even one gyration. At higher altitudes (fig. 1.10 (*a*)) the ions, being of greater mass, collide more frequently during one period of gyration than the electrons do. The influence of the magnetic field is therefore reduced and they drift in the direction of the electric field. At even higher heights (above 150 km) the ions and electrons move together so that there are no currents. This is because all charged particles there have exactly the same $\mathbf{E} \times \mathbf{B}$ drift.

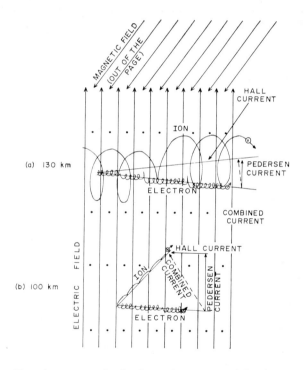

Fig. 1.10. Electric currents in the ionosphere are mainly the Pedersen and Hall currents which arise from collisions of ions and electrons with neutral particles. (*a*) At higher altitudes the ions, being of greater mass, collide more frequently during one gyration than the electrons do. A collision displaces a charged particle by the radius of one gyration on the average. (*b*) At lower altitudes collisions become so frequent that an ion cannot even complete one gyration.

21

Further reading:

Craig, R. A., 1968. *The Edge of Space.* (Garden City, N.Y.: Doubleday and Co.)

Ratcliffe, J. A., 1970. *Sun, Earth and Radio.* (London: Weidenfeld and Nicolson.)

Pushkov, N. V., and Silkin, B. I., 1968. *The Quiet Sun.* (Moscow: MIR Publishing.) (In English.)

These are at a simple non-mathematical level intended for the general reader. A book at the same level as this one is:

Goody, R. M., and Walker, J. C. G., 1972. *Atmospheres.* (Englewood Cliffs, N.J.: Prentice-Hall.)

In order to celebrate the 50th anniversary of the experiments made by Appleton and Barnett and Breit and Tuve, the December 1974 issue of the *Journal of Atmospheric and Terrestrial Physics* contains many interesting articles on the history of ionospheric research.

effects of solar radiation

2.1. *Introduction*

THE energy transmitted by the Sun primarily comes in the form of electromagnetic radiation. Most of this radiation is emitted from the photosphere, which is the thin surface layer of the Sun. The temperature in the photosphere is, on the average, 6000 K so that the near ultraviolet, visible and infrared radiation has an intensity distribution spectrum that corresponds closely with that of a 6000 K black body (fig. 2.1).

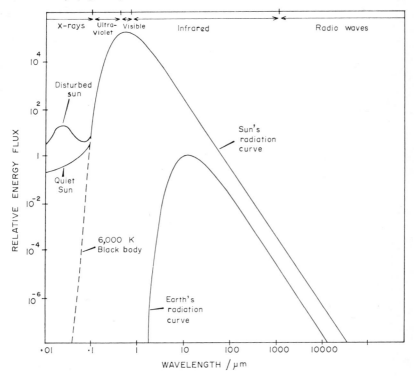

Fig. 2.1. Energy distribution curves of the Sun and Earth's radiation spectra. (Note the logarithmic scales.) The Earth emits radiation as if it were a black body near 300 K.

During a solar eclipse the main portion of the Sun is obscured by the Moon. At these times the solar corona shines like a glowing halo around the obliterated Sun. The solar corona is the tenuous outer atmosphere of the sun and it is at an exceedingly high temperature of between one and two million kelvin. X-rays and short ultra-violet rays are emitted by the corona, so that the solar spectrum for wavelengths below a few tens of nanometres approximates to that of a black body at a million kelvin. This region of the solar spectrum is usually referred to as the XUV region.

The radiation emitted from the photosphere does not change appreciably with time. However, the X-rays and far ultraviolet radiation, as well as the solar radio waves longer than 1 cm, all show a cyclic increase and decrease in intensity, with a period of 11 years. This 11-year cycle plays an important role in all solar mechanisms. During periods of high solar activity the intensity of the solar radio and XUV emission is greater, and there is a marked increase in the number of sunspots, seen as dark spots on the face of the Sun (fig. 2.2).

If the sunspots are examined in the light of the red H_α line of hydrogen (wavelength 656 nm) then a sunspot region appears brighter than the surroundings. These brighter areas are called *plages* and each corresponds well, though not exactly, with a sunspot region.

Occasionally, during periods of high solar activity, a portion of a plage area will be seen in H_α light, to brighten as a *flare*. Flares build up in one or two minutes and then decay gradually for about half an hour. Some flares emit charged particles; these exceptional events are known as proton flares and the radiation is known as solar cosmic radiation. All flares strongly emit short-wavelength X-rays.

The solar electromagnetic radiation travels at the speed of light $(3 \times 10^8$ m s$^{-1})$ and eventually reaches the Earth's atmosphere. Each species of molecule in the atmosphere has its own characteristic wavelengths at which it absorbs radiation. We say that its absorption cross-section is large at these wavelengths. Photons of sufficient quantum energy to remove an electron do so when they are absorbed, producing an electron and a positive ion.

As the radiation continues towards the Earth's surface, different atmospheric constituents absorb different wavelengths. Here ozone, O_3, which is a very minor constituent of the total atmosphere plays a very important role. Ozone in the atmosphere is mainly produced by the attachment of an oxygen atom (itself obtained from the dissociation of O_2 by ultraviolet radiation) to a diatomic oxygen molecule in the presence of a third body:

$$O + O_2 + M \rightarrow O_3 + M.$$

The ozone is concentrated in a layer centred at approximately 35 km

TEL. : 41001, EXTN. 203

DEPARTMENT OF NATURAL PHILOSOPHY
THE UNIVERSITY
DRUMMOND STREET
EDINBURGH, 8

University of Edinburgh

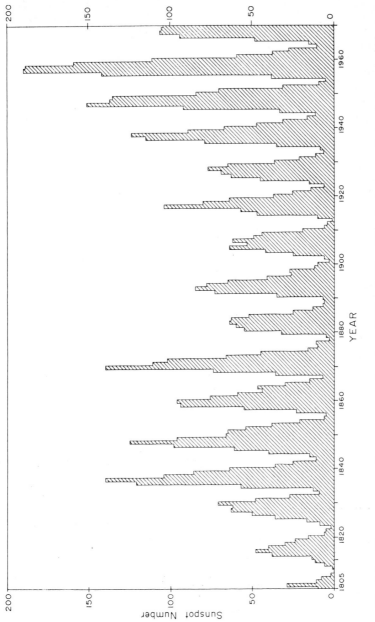

Fig. 2.2. The average yearly sunspot number from 1805 to 1970. The eleven-year solar cycle is very evident.

25

altitude. It is an efficient absorber of ultraviolet radiation between 150 nm and 300 nm and the ozone layer protects us from this range of the ultraviolet. At the same time, the absorption of this energy increases the temperature in the vicinity of the ozone layer, as explained on pages 2 and 4.

Two important bands of the electromagnetic spectrum are not significantly absorbed by any atmospheric constituent. These are visible light (wavelength range 400 nm to 600 nm) and short-wave radio waves of wavelengths 10 mm to 10 m. These bands are called the *optical window* and the *radio window* respectively. Through the marvels of biological adaptation, human eyesight developed to make the fullest use of the optical window since the Sun emits the greatest amount of radiation there.

Incoming	Absorbed by	
X-rays	O, O_2, N, N_2	Ionosphere
Ultraviolet	$O,$	Thermosphere
	O_3 (Ozone)	Stratosphere and mesosphere
Visible	(The optical window)	
Infrared	CO_2, O_3	Contributes to stratosphere
Radio	(The radio window)	Allows radio telescopes to be used
Outgoing		
Infrared	CO_2, H_2O	Troposphere

Table 2.1. Atmospheric absorption of solar radiation.

2.2. *The temperature of the Earth*

From the radiation laws and planetary data we can calculate theoretically the expected temperature of the Earth, or of any planet in the solar system.

Stefan's law states that the power per unit area emitted by a black body is proportional to the fourth power of the temperature. We know that the effective temperature of the Sun, $T_S = 5790$ K, and the mean solar radius, $R_S = 7 \cdot 0 \times 10^5$ km, so that the total power emitted by the Sun, P_S, is

$$P_S = \sigma T_S^4 \cdot 4\pi R_S^2$$

$$= 3 \cdot 92 \times 10^{26} \text{ W},$$

where $\sigma = 5 \cdot 67 \times 10^{-8}$ J m^{-2} K^{-4} s^{-1} is the Stefan–Boltzmann constant.

The Earth, of radius R_E, presents a disc of area $\pi R_E{}^2$ to the Sun so that the power falling as radiation on the Earth, P_E, is given by

$$P_E = \frac{P_S}{4\pi D_{ES}{}^2} \cdot \pi R_E{}^2$$

where $D_{ES} = 1{\cdot}5 \times 10^8$ km is the mean distance between the Earth and the Sun (see fig. 2.3).

The quantity $P_S/4\pi D_{ES}{}^2$ is the amount of energy, of all wavelengths, incident in unit time on unit area of a surface placed at right angles to the Sun's rays at the Earth's mean distance from the Sun. This quantity is called the solar constant and it has a value of $1{\cdot}39$ kW m^{-2}. We shall assume that this energy/power is all absorbed.

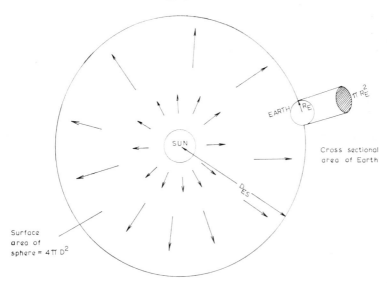

Fig. 2.3. The Earth absorbs a fraction $\pi R_E{}^2/4\pi D^2$ of the total power emitted by the Sun.

As we assume that the Earth acts like a black body then the power absorbed by the Earth is re-radiated, at a temperature T_E, in accordance with Stefan's Law. Thus,

Total power re-radiated by the Earth $= \sigma T_E{}^4 \cdot 4\pi R_E{}^2$

$$= P_E = P_S \cdot \pi R_E{}^2/4\pi D_{ES}{}^2$$

so that

$$T_E = T_s \sqrt{\left(\frac{R_S}{2D_{ES}} \right)}$$

$$\approx 280 \text{ K}$$

27

Similar calculations can be made for the other planets of the solar system giving, for example, mean temperatures of 325 K for Venus and 225 K for Mars. These temperatures are not necessarily related to the actual temperatures since we have assumed that the planets are black bodies. This is a reasonably good assumption for the Earth but Venus seems to reflect a great deal of the incident radiation.

The surface temperatures of many planets, however, tend to be higher than the theoretical mean temperature. Earth has a maximum surface temperature of 310 K, Mars 250 K and Venus an extremely high surface temperature of up to 700 K. The reason for these high temperatures is that the carbon dioxide and water vapour in these planets' atmospheres acts like a blanket and traps the outgoing infrared radiation.*

There was a steady rise of about 2 K per decade in the Earth's mean surface temperature for the first half of this century. Some people attribute this to the increased amounts of carbon dioxide pumped into the atmosphere by the cars and factories which symbolize the industrial society. Others claim that this is merely part of a natural long-term cycle of temperature changes. Most of the more recent evidence tends to support the second viewpoint since the mean surface temperature has recently been falling, but it is a sobering thought to realize just how important the minor constituents of the atmosphere are, and to contemplate some of the possible risks from atmospheric pollution that may face us.

The horizontal patterns of temperature from the equator to the poles also exhibit striking peculiarities (fig. 2.4). At the Earth's surface, temperatures decrease from the equator to the poles, and a comparable decrease holds true for the lowest 10 km of the atmosphere. At the 15 to 20 kilometre level, however, the situation is reversed. Temperatures of about 200 K can be found over the Equator all the year round, whereas temperatures over the Arctic vary between 210 K in winter to 230 K in summer.

Let us imagine an Eskimo equipped with a magic carpet travelling from the North Pole to the South Pole in July at an altitude of 20 km. We can follow his journey on fig. 2.4 by moving along the 20 km height level from the summer to the winter hemisphere (left to right). The temperature at 20 km over the North Pole in July is around 240 K. This is about the temperature the Eskimo would be used to in winter on the Earth's surface. As the magic carpet heads towards the Equator, our unfortunate Eskimo finds that he keeps having to pile on more and more furs. By the time he reaches the Equator the temperature is a staggering 190 K ($-83°C$). If he survives this cold then he will be cheered up by the slight increase in temperature as he

* Dust storms on Mars also help to raise that planet's temperature. The dust absorbs solar radiation and helps to warm up the atmosphere.

continues south. By the time he reaches the South Pole it will be 220 K. Not as warm as the North Pole, but a lot warmer than the Equator. However, if the flying Eskimo had invested in a super carpet capable of flying at 50 km altitude then he could have done the whole journey in temperatures that he would be used to on the Earth's surface.

In the stratosphere between 25 and 50 km, temperatures decrease toward the winter pole and increase toward the summer pole. This is to be expected; the winter pole receives no solar radiation during the long polar night and the summer pole is continuously heated by the Sun. Paradoxically, in the next highest region, between 50 and 80 km, recorded temperatures swing directly opposite to expectation. In the middle of winter, mesospheric temperatures over the pole appear to be scarcely lower than at the polar surface: about 240 K. In summer, when the Sun is shining steadily on the pole, the temperature at about 80 km can plummet to as low as 130 K, the lowest temperature yet recorded in the Earth's atmosphere.

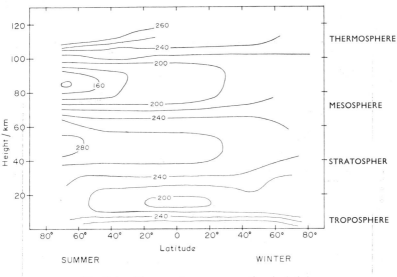

Fig. 2.4. Temperature cross section in kelvins.

This curious behaviour of the polar mesosphere is still not completely understood. It does indicate, however, that direct absorption of solar radiation does not take place in the mesosphere as it does in the stratosphere where ozone absorbs strongly, and where temperatures follow expectations. Thus, the clue to the mesospheric temperature puzzle must lie in winds or other air movements transporting heat from one place to another.

2.3. *Formation of the ionosphere*

We have already seen that the Earth's atmosphere is a mixture of a number of different species of gaseous molecules, each with its own characteristic absorption. It is obvious that if some of the incident radiation is absorbed near the top of the atmosphere, only the remainder will be available to ionize the particles lower down. Let us consider one particular kind of particle, and one particular ionizing wavelength, for this discussion at first.

At the very top of the atmosphere there are very few particles so little of the incoming ionizing radiation is absorbed at first. As it penetrates further down, there is a greater density of neutral un-ionized particles and more and more absorption takes place. So the ionosphere that forms is determined by the balance between the intensity of the incoming radiation, which decreases as one goes down, and the density of ionizable material, which decreases as one goes up. At a certain height the rate at which the gas concentration *increases* downwards will be matched by the rate at which the strength of the radiation *decreases* downwards. So, at this height, the rate of production of electrons would be greatest and this level is called the peak

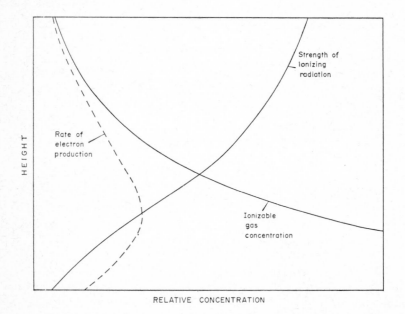

Fig. 2.5. A Chapman layer (dotted line) of electrons forms when the strength of the ionizing radiations, which decreases downwards, is balanced by the amount of the atmosphere available for ionization, which increases downwards.

of the ionospheric layer (fig. 2.5). The same thing indeed happens for the other species present, and the appropriate wavelengths.

The theory was worked out by Sydney Chapman (1888–1970), and the ideal ionospheric layer that we have described is called a Chapman layer. The height and the rate of production of ionization of a Chapman layer are strongly influenced by the solar zenith angle χ. This is the angle that the Sun makes with the vertical. The solar zenith angle decreases during the morning, reaching its minimum value at noon and then it increases during the afternoon. Its value depends both on the time of year and the location at which it is being measured. During midwinter in London, England, χ is always greater than $75°$.

The absorption of radiation follows Beer's Law. If radiation of given wavelength and intensity I is absorbed by a gas of particle concentration $\mathcal{N}$ then the change in intensity in a distance $\mathrm{d}l$ is proportional to $\mathcal{N}$ and to $\mathrm{d}l$ and to I itself, so that

$$\mathrm{d}I = -Iv\mathcal{N}\,\mathrm{d}l$$

where v (which has units m^2) is termed the absorption cross-section. It is not a direct measure of the cross-sectional area of a gas molecule but is a measure of how strongly a particular wavelength is absorbed, and so v varies with the wavelength of the radiation as well as with the nature of the gas.

Chapman assumed that the amount of energy absorbed per unit volume is proportional to the number of electrons produced in this volume. The constant of proportionality, η (units: number of particles per watt) is called the ionizing efficiency. Chapman's assumption can then be represented mathematically by

$$q = \eta\frac{\mathrm{d}I}{\mathrm{d}l}$$

where q is the rate of ionization production per unit volume. But from Beer's law

$$q = -\eta v\mathcal{N}I.$$

and we can use Beer's law again to find I in terms of $\mathcal{N}$. But, provided we know the scale height, then we can find $\mathcal{N}$ as a function of altitude, so we then have q as a function of altitude. Chapman did this and showed that the height of the peak of a Chapman layer, h_{m}, does not depend on the strength of the incoming radiation but is given by the formula

$$h_{\mathrm{m}} = H\log_e(\mathcal{N}_0 vH\sec\chi)$$

where $\mathcal{N}_0$ is the neutral gas concentration (number of particles per unit volume) *at the ground* and H is the scale height of the gas.

31

The rate of production of ionization per unit volume, on the other hand, has a peak that does not depend on $\mathcal{N}$, the amount of neutral gas. It is given by the formula

Maximum rate of ionization production per unit volume =

$$q_{max} = \eta \frac{I \cos \chi}{2 \cdot 72 \, H}$$

In fig. 2.6 (*a*) we can see that during the morning, as χ decreases, the Chapman layer gets bigger and descends. Though it is not immediately obvious, the shape of the layer always stays the same. If we redraw the curves of fig. 2.6 (*a*) so that the maximum production rate is always at unity and the height of the peak is taken as zero, then the single curve of fig. 2.6 (*b*) describes all the curves of the earlier diagram.

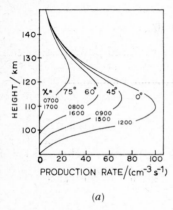 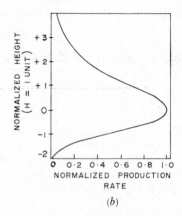

(*a*) (*b*)

Fig. 2.6. (*a*) A Chapman layer at Accra, Ghana during the equinoxes. (*b*) Chapman layers in normalized units can all be represented by one curve. All the layers of fig. 2.6 (*a*) will be found to correspond to this one.

The formation of real ionospheric layers can be closely represented on Chapman's theory provided a careful analysis is made of all the species available for ionization, the ionizing wavelengths available and their penetrating power. The subsequent behaviour of real layers, once they are formed, depends on the loss processes that destroy the ionization, which is in turn dependent on the chemistry of the upper atmosphere. The next section looks at this. In practice the E region can be almost exactly described by the simple Chapman theory given above. The F region properties can be predicted by a Chapman layer that is strongly controlled by diffusion and recombination, but the D region is so chemically complex that the simple Chapman theory cannot be used for it at all.

One might well think that during winter at the North and South Poles there could be no ionosphere since there is no solar radiation shining on the atmosphere in the land of midday darkness. In fact there is an ionosphere with rather normal properties. The main reason for this is that there is a steady invasion of particles sliding down the magnetic field lines from the radiation belts. These particles guarantee the existence of the polar ionosphere.

2.4. Atomic and molecular reactions

The upper atmospheric reactions that are important will vary depending on the height range that is being studied. We shall deal with the reactions that take place in the ionosphere and in the ozone layer. However, different chemical reactions dominate in the upper and lower parts of the ionosphere and it is this difference which is responsible in large part for separate E and F regions.

The E region

The two dominant ions in the 90–150 km height range are O_2^+ and NO^+. Despite the preponderance of molecular nitrogen, N_2, in the atmosphere there is a scarcity of N_2^+ ions in all regions of the ionosphere since they react very quickly with oxygen.

The predominant mechanism responsible for loss of ionization in this part of the lower ionosphere is one of dissociative recombination. Primarily

$$① : NO^+ + e \longrightarrow N + O$$
$$② : O_2^+ + e \longrightarrow O + O$$

The nature of the ionosphere will depend on the rates at which these reactions take place. The reaction rate depends on the number of electrons per unit volume, N, and the number of ions per unit volume. Even though N should properly be called the electron concentration it is conventional to refer to it as the electron density. If we denote the number of ionized molecules by N_m, then the loss rate, L, is proportional to both the number of electrons and to the number of ionized molecules so

$$L = \alpha N N_m$$

where α is called the recombination coefficient. Typical values of α are about 5×10^{-13} m^3 s^{-1} throughout the E region.

The F region

In the upper regions of the ionosphere, above 150 km, ultraviolet radiation with wavelength below 250 nm breaks the molecular oxygen into atomic oxygen.

$$O_2 + hf \rightarrow O + O \quad (\lambda < 250 \text{ nm}).$$

This dissociation reaction is a *photodissociation* reaction, and it is this particular photodissociation of molecular oxygen that is responsible for the fact that the concentration of O in the F region is greater than the concentration of O_2 (fig. 2.7).

For a given wavelength λ (in m) the photon energy, E (in J), is given in terms of the Planck constant, $h = 6.63 \times 10^{-34}$ J s, the speed of light $c = 3.00 \times 10^8$ m s^{-1} and the frequency f (in Hz) as

$$E = hf = hc/\lambda.$$

Atomic oxygen ions do not recombine well with electrons, and in the F region the atomic oxygen ions undergo a charge-transfer reaction

$$③ : O^+ + N_2 \rightarrow NO^+ + N \rightarrow \text{reaction } ①$$
$$④ : O^+ + O_2 \rightarrow O_2^+ + O \rightarrow \text{reaction } ②$$

and after the charge transfer has been completed then the same dissociative recombination takes place as in the E region.

In fact all the reactions ①, ②, ③ and ④ are going on at all heights in the ionosphere. The controlling reaction is the *slowest*

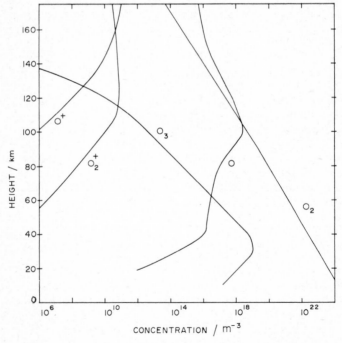

Fig. 2.7. Daytime concentration of atmospheric oxygen.

one. Thus in the E region there is very little O^+, and the little that there is undergoes charge-transfer reactions so quickly that it is difficult to detect.

The loss rate for the charge-transfer process will be proportional to the number density of atomic ions N_a, and to the number of neutral gas particles, $\mathcal{N}$, so

$$L = \gamma \mathcal{N} N_a$$

where γ is a constant of proportionality. It is more usual to write this in the form

$$L = \beta N_a$$

where β is called the attachment-like coefficient. Since $\mathcal{N}$ decreases exponentially with height, β will also decrease with height. It has a value of about 10^{-4} s^{-1} at 300 km and decreases upwards with height z in kilometres according to the equation

$$\beta = 10^{-4} \exp \left[(300 - z)/50\right]$$

Reaction dynamics

During the daytime a large part of the ionosphere is in equilibrium. The rate of production of ionization equals the rate of loss of ionization.

Since the ions are undergoing all the reactions ① to ④, at equilibrium

$$q = \beta N_a$$

for the charge-transfer process and

$$q = \alpha N N_m$$

for the dissociative recombination.

However, the number of electrons must equal the total number of ions since the atmosphere has no overall electric charge, so

$$N = N_a + N_m$$

$$= \frac{q}{\beta} + \frac{q}{\alpha N}$$

and we do not have to know the number of molecular or atomic ions present but can use only the electron density, in terms of which

$$\frac{1}{q} = \frac{1}{\beta N} + \frac{1}{\alpha N^2}$$

if $\beta \gg \alpha N$, as is the case in the E region, then $q = \alpha N^2$ and $N_m \gg N_a$. Conversely if $\beta \ll \alpha N$, as in the F region, then $q = \beta N$ and $N_a \gg N_m$.

We already know a value for q at the peak of the layer. From Chapman's theory we know that $q_{max} \propto \cos \chi$, so that this enables us to decide how closely a real ionospheric layer approximates to an ideal Chapman layer.

If the E region behaves like a Chapman layer then the number density of electrons in the peak should vary with the solar zenith angle as $N \propto \sqrt{(\cos \chi)}$. If the F region behaves like a Chapman layer then at the F region peak $N \propto \cos \chi$.

Radio observations using ionosondes show that the E region does indeed behave much like a Chapman layer in which there is equilibrium between the rate of production of electrons and the rate of loss. The F region peak, however, does not have its electron density proportional to $\cos \chi$. This is not because Chapman's theory is incorrect, but because we have not taken into account the strong movements of the ionization in the F region which make it incorrect to assume that during any interval exactly the same number of electrons are produced as are lost through recombination. The transport of electrons and ions can produce more, or less, ionization at any chosen location than the idea of a simple balance would predict.

The ozone layer

The ozone layer is responsible for the positive upward temperature gradient in the stratosphere due to the absorption of ultraviolet radiation with wavelengths below 300 nm. The amount of ozone in the stratosphere is thus intimately connected to the stratospheric temperature. This is especially evident during periods of stratospheric warming in which the temperature may rise tens of kelvins above its normal seasonal value and stay at a high value for some days, and in which there is a marked increase in the ozone content. Stratospheric warmings also offer evidence of a linkage between the ionosphere and the stratosphere since noticeable changes in the ionosphere are also observed during stratospheric warmings.

Ozone is formed by the three-body collision

$$O + O_2 + M \rightarrow O_3 + M$$

The constituent M may be any neutral atom or molecule, and though it remains chemically unchanged, its kinetic energy and momentum will change. The reason that the third body, M, is needed is that it is impossible to satisfy both energy conservation and momentum conservation in a two-body reaction.

The atomic oxygen required for the production of the ozone is obtained from the photodissociation of molecular oxygen by wavelengths below 250 nm.

$$O_2 + hf \rightarrow O + O \quad (\lambda < 250 \text{ nm})$$

36

Once the ozone is formed it can be destroyed by two types of reaction, either by collisions with atomic oxygen

$$O_3 + O \rightarrow 2O_2$$

or by photodissociation produced by wavelengths less than $1 \cdot 1 \, \mu m$

$$O_3 + hf \rightarrow O + O_2 \quad (\lambda < 1 \cdot 1 \, \mu m)$$

The ozone below the peak of the ozone layer at 30 km is protected from dissociation by the large amounts of ozone above (fig. 2.7). Because of this the ozone below 30 km can be used as a tracer. By knowing the seasonal and latitudinal variations of ozone, the stratospheric circulation can be studied. The lower atmosphere gains ozone from the stratosphere by large-scale mixing near the tropopause, and the study of this is of considerable importance because radioactive debris deposited in the stratosphere by nuclear explosions enters the lower atmosphere in exactly the same way that ozone does.

The advent of supersonic aircraft that fly in the stratosphere has aroused some concern over the possible depletion of the ozone layer. The problem is that the exhaust gases contain oxides of nitrogen, NO and NO_2. Under laboratory conditions it is known that these nitrogen oxides convert ozone into molecular oxygen. The danger is that this may also occur in the stratosphere, depleting the ozone layer and so increasing the amount of ultraviolet radiation reaching the Earth's surface. A certain amount of optimism is possible however, since the large number of atmospheric nuclear tests exploded in the past three decades have all released sizeable concentrations of NO and NO_2 into the stratosphere without significantly affecting the ozone layer.

Another possible danger to the ozone layer stems from aerosol spray cans. The chemicals used in these as propellant are fluorocarbons (also known as Freon), CF_2Cl_2 and $CFCl_3$, which are chemically inert in the lower atmosphere. The danger is that they will be carried up to the ozone layer by the atmosphere's normal turbulent mixing and be decomposed into a free chlorine atom which can react with ozone:

$$Cl + O_3 \rightarrow ClO + O_2$$

The 1972 world production rates for the fluorocarbons were already large enough to have major effects on the ozone level if, or when, they are completely mixed into the troposphere and stratosphere. And production since 1972 has been expanding. The American National Academy of Science has created a special panel to investigate these effects. We may yet see aerosol spray cans banned.

2.5. *Minor constituents*

We have seen that the presence of minor constituents affects the upper atmosphere in many ways. Sometimes though, constituents that are highly important in the lower atmosphere, such as CO_2, do not seem to play a role in the upper atmosphere. Similarly, hydrogen and helium are also unimportant except at the uppermost reaches of the atmosphere above 500 km.

Nitric oxide

The problem of nitric oxide interfering with the ozone layer has already been dealt with. Natural un-ionized nitric oxide is a very minor constituent whose production depends on the concentration of atomic nitrogen, since it is formed by

$$N + O_2 \rightarrow NO + O$$

Most of the atomic nitrogen in the atmosphere comes from the ultra-violet dissociation of N_2, but at the heights where this is important most of the O_2 is also being dissociated to atomic oxygen and not much nitric oxide forms. In fact the atomic nitrogen responsible for producing nitric oxide comes from the charge exchange reaction ③ discussed in the previous section. The amount of atomic nitrogen below 80 km drops rapidly so that any nitric oxide found there will have been transported down.

Nitric oxide is crucial in developing the lowest ionospheric region, the D region, since the Lyman-α radiation at 121·6 nm ionizes only NO. The upper atmosphere above 90 km acts as a window for Lyman-α radiation which arrives undiminished on the D region. Even though incoming solar X rays and cosmic rays ionize all atmospheric gases at all levels down to and including the D region, the extra ionization obtained from NO is really responsible for the existence of a complete ionospheric layer under the main body of the ionosphere.

Nitric oxide has a lifetime of the order of a few days so that once formed it remains in the atmosphere for quite long periods. At night in the D region, O and N concentrations drop markedly and NO becomes the dominant minor constituent.

Water vapour

The role of water vapour in the upper atmosphere interests us because of the visual display that occurs when clouds form. Mother-of-pearl clouds are sometimes seen around 25 km altitude, but during summer very high clouds are sometimes visible at the mesopause. Since nightfall at 80 km occurs much later than it does on the ground, and daylight is correspondingly earlier, these very high clouds are called noctilucent clouds since they are visible during periods of night time on the earth's surface. The normal water vapour content of the atmosphere can explain the mother-of-pearl clouds but noctilucent clouds are more difficult to explain. At noctilucent cloud heights radiation dissociates the water vapour

$$H_2O + hf \rightarrow H^+ + OH^-$$

and reduces the water vapour content well below that necessary to produce clouds. Thus there must be either an upward transport of water vapour, or a source of water vapour, or both. Which of these mechanisms occurs and the exact nature of any possible water vapour source is still uncertain. The problem is further compounded by the recent discovery that the chief positive ions in the D region are water cluster ions $H^+(H_2O)_n$ with $H_5O_2^+$ generally predominant. The photodissociation of methane in the presence of oxygen has been suggested as a likely source mechanism.

There is also a temperature problem. To form clouds low temperatures are needed and this is why noctilucent clouds occur at the mesopause. During summer the mesopause can cool to 130 K, when clouds may be found; however in winter the mesopause temperature remains above 200 K, which is contrary to expectations based on radiative equilibrium. The most plausible suggestion so far views the air at the winter mesopause as descending. During its descent it heats adiabatically and it converts its atomic oxygen to molecular oxygen. The adiabatic heating and the heat released by the chemical reaction might be sufficient to account for the high winter temperature.

Metallic ions

Various heavy ions are observed in the E region by mass spectrometers carried by rockets. These are principally Na^+, Mg^+, Fe^+ and Ca^+. It is generally believed that these metals are deposited in the E region during the vaporization of meteors, the high temperatures during vaporization being responsible also for the ionization of the metals. Since most meteors, which start as very small bits of extraterrestrial matter, vaporize at E region heights the metallic ions are found to be in a thin layer, less than 10 km thick, centred at about 90 km altitude.

Metallic ions have extremely long lifetimes, and can exist as ions for up to two days before recombining with an electron.

Negative ions

If you talk about ionization to a chemist he will point out that it is easier for oxygen to produce negative ions by allowing a neutral molecule to capture an electron than it is to produce positive ions. To create positive (O^+, O_2^+) ions one needs to supply energy whereas the creation of negative (O^-, O_2^-) ions releases energy.

In the lower parts of the ionosphere we find negative ions. In the E and F regions we do not, because any free electrons recombine with positive ions more quickly than they can find a neutral molecule to join. In the D region though, there is a much greater density of neutral molecules so that a free electron will be able to collide with a neutral molecule and attach itself to it before it has time to recombine with a positive ion.

Since nitrogen does not form stable negative ions, O^- and O_2^- are probably the most common negative ions, formed respectively by

$$O + e \rightarrow O^- + hf$$

and

$$M + O_2 + e \rightarrow O_2^- + M$$

Data obtained by the absorption of radio waves crossing the polar regions during periods of unusually high radio wave absorption (generally abbreviated as PCA = polar cap absorption) indicates that some other negative ions, most probably O_3^- and NO_2^-, must also exist.

Hydroxyl

The presence of hydroxyl radicals in the upper atmosphere is dependent on the existence and distribution of ozone and atomic hydrogen:

$$O_3 + H \rightarrow OH + O_2$$

The hydroxyl radical thus formed is in an excited state and it decays to its ground state by emitting radiation strongly in the infrared, especially from $2 \cdot 8 \, \mu$m to $4 \cdot 0 \, \mu$m. This radiation is an important part of the airglow spectrum.

2.6. *Airglow*

When a photon of radiation, and especially very short wavelength radiation, is absorbed by a gas molecule it may do one of a number of things. We have seen that the molecule can be ionized, or dissociated so that smaller molecules or atoms form. Furthermore the molecule may be excited by being raised from its lowest energy state (ground state) into some higher energy state. Also, the dissociation process may produce new atoms or molecules which are in an excited state. When an excited particle relaxes to its ground state, energy is released. Some of this energy is radiated away as light—as airglow.

40

As might be expected, airglow is most intense by day; but then it is almost impossible to observe against the general bright sky background except by making measurements from rockets or satellites which climb above the heights where scattering produces a bright sky background. Airglow continues with only slightly reduced intensity throughout the night when it can be measured and analysed at the ground. The transition from day to night, or vice versa, is noticeable on airglow spectra because at twilight the upper atmosphere is being illuminated from below (fig. 2.8) and the spectrum obtained differs from both the day and night spectra. Because of this it is usual to talk of dayglow, nightglow and twilightglow separately.

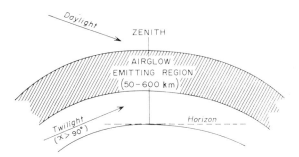

Fig. 2.8. Twilightglow differs from dayglow because different regions of the atmosphere, containing different constituents, are illuminated by the Sun.

At the ground the total luminance from airglow is about the same as the total luminance from all the stars. When the radiation is examined spectroscopically it is seen to contain a large number of discrete spectral lines as well as a number of bands of closely spaced lines. Each of these lines and bands arises from some definite photochemical reaction or some definite excitation change and the sources of many of these airglow lines have now been identified (Table 2.2.) The sources of some others still remain a mystery.

The processes of excitation, whereby an atom or a molecule absorbs energy that is subsequently emitted as radiation, are of five kinds. I will list these mechanisms, including examples. Some of the examples we will have met before, but this time we will specially note when a reaction produces an excited particle. To emphasize the excitations I will follow the normal convention and represent an excited particle by an asterisk.

(i) Ionic excitation: this occurs when an ion is in an excited state and decays to its ground state without losing its ionization. For example, the photoionization of nitrogen molecules leaves them in an

41

	Wavelength nm	Day glow	Twilight glow	Night glow
Hydrogen (H)				
*Lyman-α	121·6	x	x	x
H_α	656·3			x
Oxygen (O)				
Green line	557·7	x	x	x
Red line	630·0 & 636·4	x	x	x
Oxygen (O_2)				
Herzberg band	250·0 to 400·0			x
Kaplan–Meinel band	864·5	x		x
*Infrared ⎱	761·9	x		x
system ⎰	1270·0	x	x	x
Nitrogen ($N_2{}^+$)				
0–0 band	391·4	x	x	
0–1 band	427·8		x	
Sodium (Na)				
D lines	589·0 & 589·6	x	x	x
Calcium (Ca^+)				
K line	393·3		x	
Hydroxyl (OH)				
Meinel band	2800 to 4000			x
Unknown (NO_2?)				
Continuum	370·0 to 900·0			x

Table 2.2. Principal airglow emissions. The emissions indicated by asterisks are not visible at the ground because they are absorbed before reaching the ground.

excited state which decays to its ground state just before the $N_2{}^+$ interacts with oxygen:

$$N_2 + hf \rightarrow N_2{}^{+*} \xrightarrow[\text{427·8 nm}]{\text{391·4 nm}} N_2{}^+$$

This process is only going to operate during the daytime when there are incoming photons to simultaneously ionize and excite the atoms and molecules.

(ii) Recombination: Recombination reactions are important in controlling ionospheric dynamics. In addition, the reaction

$$O_2{}^+ + e \rightarrow O^* + O^* \xrightarrow[\text{636·4 nm}]{\text{630·0 nm}} O + O$$

produces the red line of oxygen, during both day and night, when the excited states of oxygen return to their ground level.

(iii) Chemiluminescence: this is the most common form of airglow, which occurs when atmospheric chemical reactions result in the emission of photons. The green line of oxygen comes from

$$O + O + O \rightarrow O_2 + O^* \xrightarrow{\quad 557 \cdot 7 \text{ nm} \quad} O_2 + O$$

as do the Herzberg bands which arise from the three-body reaction

$$M + O + O \rightarrow O_2^* + M \xrightarrow[\quad 400 \text{ nm} \quad]{\quad 250 \text{ nm} \quad} O_2 + M$$

(Remember, M may be any neutral atom or molecule.) In addition most of the chemical reactions involving the minor constituents, Na^+, Ca^+, OH produce airglow from chemiluminescence.

(iv) Resonance and fluorescence: Resonance scattering is the absorption and emission of photons without a change in the photon energy, i.e. radiation is absorbed and re-emitted without a change in the wavelength. Fluorescence in the absorption of photons of one energy and the emission of photons of lesser energy; radiation of one wavelength is absorbed and radiation of a longer wavelength is emitted.

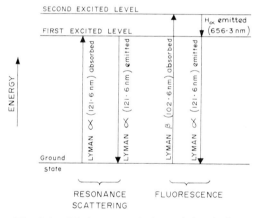

Fig. 2.9.   Hydrogen emissions of the airglow.

The atomic hydrogen emissions of the airglow (fig. 2.9) demonstrate these two phenomena. In resonance scattering, a hydrogen atom in the ground state absorbs a photon of the incoming solar (Lyman-α) radiation, is excited to the first excited state and then, after a certain interval of time, re-emits a photon of the same energy to return to the ground state.

43

On the other hand if a photon of the incoming Lyman-β radiation is absorbed, raising the atom to the second excited state, then de-excitation occurs by the emission of two photons whose total energy equals, or is less than the energy of the incoming photon. This is fluorescence. In the hydrogen atom the energy of the hydrogen α photon and the Lyman-α photon do in fact total the energy of the Lyman-β photon. But, if the absorbed photon causes ionization then part or all of the energy of the incoming photon will be carried away by the electron.

Fluorescence is also generated in the upper atmosphere by cosmic X-rays of solar or stellar origin. They liberate electrons from atmospheric atoms and molecules at an altitude of about 80 km. The electrons in turn ionize and excite molecular nitrogen to form N_2^+, which emits the band at 391·4 nm that is such a strong feature of the twilight glow. Observations of this fluorescence have been used to detect the detonation of nuclear weapons in the atmosphere, since the weapons also generate X-rays.

(v) Inelastic collisions: Fast charged particles can excite atoms or molecules by giving up a small amount of energy on impact and exciting the atom or molecule to a higher energy state, or by simultaneously ionizing and exciting molecules. We have seen that this type of reaction was a by-product of the X-ray fluorescence of upper atmospheric particles when the liberated electrons interact with nitrogen

$$N_2 + e \rightarrow N_2^{+*} + 2e \xrightarrow{\text{391·4 nm}} N_2^+ + 2e$$

The direct inelastic collision of electrons and atoms or molecules is not a dominant process in the airglow though a weak line in the twilight glow is caused by the inelastic collision of an electron and atomic helium

$$He + e \rightarrow He^* + e \xrightarrow{\text{1083 nm}} He + e$$

In addition to these five processes, another process called quenching must be taken into account. An excited atom or molecule does not always lose its energy by emitting radiation; an event such as a collision with another particle can de-excite it. This is called *quenching*.

Artificial airglow

The intensity of the natural airglow is low; it is barely perceptible by the unaided eye. But if the concentration of any of the responsible gases can be deliberately increased, for example by injection from a rocket, or if some entirely new but active gas can be introduced,

44

then there will be a local increase in the brightness of the corresponding airglow emission. If this experiment is carried out at twilight, at a time when the released vapour is in sunlight, and so is excited by solar radiation but the lower atmosphere is in darkness, then the resulting glow, seen against a dark sky background, can be very

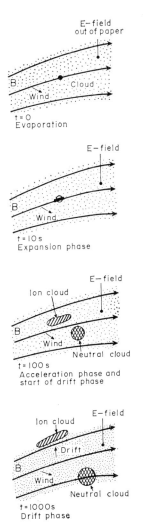

Fig. 2.10. When barium is injected into the upper atmosphere it expands and part of it becomes ionized. The purple ions move differently from the green neutrals. This allows the wind and the electric field to be determined.

bright indeed. Such glows can persist at heights between 90 and 400 km for tens of minutes. At levels up to 200 km the movements of the glow, or perhaps of a continuous trial, can provide a good indicator of winds and turbulence. It was by analysing sodium vapour trails deposited by rockets that the existence of the turbopause was discovered. Below 100 km the vapour trail would be quickly distorted by turbulence whereas above 110 km the trail remained smooth for long periods.

Recent experiments have been injecting rather more exotic chemicals that are not normally present in the atmosphere. One of the most useful chemicals is barium vapour, which emits a greenish-yellow light and moves with the neutral wind. However, barium is quickly ionized by incident sunlight and the ionized barium glows purple. The ionized atoms are constrained by the Earth's magnetic field and the purple ionized cloud is elongated along a magnetic field line. The neutral atoms move freely with the wind remaining as a more or less spherical cloud, and become separated from the ionized cloud (fig. 2.10). Since the drift of the ionized cloud is controlled by the atmosphere's electric field, information is obtained about the winds and the electric and magnetic fields. In addition, a precise examination of the emission lines and the relative strengths of related lines can determine the temperature, and identification of the excitation processes responsible for the particular emissions observed tell us something about the constitution of the atmosphere at these high levels. Barium clouds released by satellites can give us similar information about the magnetosphere.

Further reading:

Bates, D. R., 1970. Reactions in the ionosphere, *Contemporary Physics*, **11,** 105–124.
Frith, R., 1968. The Earth's high atmosphere, *Weather*, **23,** 142–155.
Ingham, M. F., 1972. The spectrum of the airglow, *Scientific American*, **226** (1), 78–85.
Lust, R., 1972. Space experiments with barium clouds, *New Scientist*, **53,** 154–157.

These are all written at the same level as this chapter, though they deal with each subject in greater depth. More advanced reference books on solar radiation are:

Goody, R. M., 1964. *Atmospheric Radiation.* (Oxford: University Press.)
Kondratyev, K. Ya., 1969. *Radiation in the Atmosphere.* (New York: Academic Press.)

CHAPTER 3
atmospheric motions

3.1. *Introduction*

IF there is a region of high pressure at one location, and a region of low pressure at another location then air will flow under the influence of pressure difference. At the same time, a mass of moving air is acted on by other external forces of which the two most important are gravity, and the Coriolis force which arises from the Earth's rotation.

Air is usually in equilibrium with gravity. We have called this hydrostatic equilibrium and seen that it leads to a continuous upward decrease of pressure. A lower pressure on top of a higher pressure results in an upward force, but in hydrostatic equilibrium this force is just balanced by the downward force of gravity. Departures from hydrostatic equilibrium are normally small, but the large departures which can sometimes occur produce spectacularly strong winds like hurricanes and typhoons. These occur because of the friction between the Earth's surface and the air, but they are not possible above 1 km altitude and are definitely not important in the upper atmosphere.

The Coriolis force deflects the air because we are looking at it from a rotating Earth. For example, if you make a straight scratch from the centre of a gramophone record to the needle whilst the record is rotating on the turntable then you will find a curved line on the gramophone record when you stop the turntable and examine it

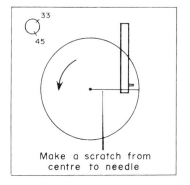

Make a scratch from centre to needle

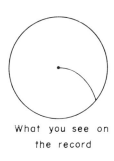

What you see on the record

Fig. 3.1.   The Coriolis force at work.

(fig. 3.1). Any little green men living on the surface of the gramophone record would have reasoned like this:

We know that Newton's first law tells us that bodies move in a straight line unless some external force acts. The body making the scratch did not move in a straight line so that apparently some external force, which we shall call the Coriolis force, must have been acting.

We are in the same position as those little green men except that we live on a rotating sphere instead of a rotating disc. The magnitude of the deflecting force on air moving on the Earth's surface (or on a disc's surface) is proportional to the angular velocity of the Earth (or the turntable) and to the speed of the wind (or the speed of the body making the scratch).

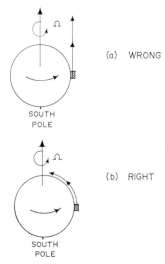

Fig. 3.2. (a) Air obeying Newton's first law being moved in a straight line. (b) Gravity overcomes the vertical Coriolis force.

We must be careful when we apply the Coriolis force to the Earth. If we are not careful, we would say that a parcel of air moving from the Equator to the North Pole will continue in a straight line when viewed from the Moon. In other words the air will continue on into space because, as our little green men would say, there is a vertical component of the Coriolis force. This is wrong because gravity is much stronger than the vertical Coriolis force and makes sure that we do not have apparent vertical motions by maintaining hydrostatic equilibrium (once again). This is illustrated in fig. 3.2.

Of course the air moving from the Equator to the North Pole is deflected horizontally. The horizontal deflecting force depends on

48

the vertical component of the Earth's angular velocity, which is $\Omega_E \sin \phi$ at any latitude ϕ. The horizontal Coriolis force, $\mathbf{F}_C$, acting on mass, m, of air has a magnitude

$$F_C = 2mU\Omega_E \sin \phi$$

where U is the speed of the wind. The direction of the Coriolis force can be found as follows. $\Omega_E \sin \phi$ is the vertical (axis) vector symbolizing angular velocity. It points vertically upwards in the northern hemisphere and vertically downwards in the southern hemisphere where ϕ is negative. So that in rotating from the direction toward which U is blowing to the direction of $\Omega_E \sin \phi$ we should imagine that we are turning a right-handed screw which will move in the direction of the Coriolis force (fig. 3.3).

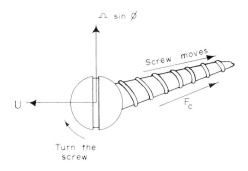

Fig. 3.3. The direction of the Coriolis force.

Thus, in summary, we have seen that the winds are determined by the three external forces acting on the air—gravity, the Coriolis force and the pressure gradient force. If we want to write this mathematically, then Newton's second law becomes, for unit volume

$$(x) \quad \rho \frac{\mathrm{d}U_x}{\mathrm{d}t} = -\frac{\mathrm{d}p}{\mathrm{d}x} + \mathscr{F}U_y\rho \qquad (3.1)$$

$$(y) \quad \rho \frac{\mathrm{d}U_y}{\mathrm{d}t} = -\frac{\mathrm{d}p}{\mathrm{d}y} - \mathscr{F}U_x\rho \qquad (3.2)$$

$$\left(\begin{matrix}\text{Hydrostatic}\\\text{equilibrium}\end{matrix}\right) (z) \quad 0 = -\frac{\mathrm{d}p}{\mathrm{d}z} - \rho g \quad (3.3)$$

| time rate of change of momentum per unit volume | pressure gradient forces per unit volume | Coriolis deflecting forces per unit volume | weight |

where $\mathscr{F} = 2\Omega_E \sin \phi$ is called the Coriolis parameter. We take x as eastward, y as northward and z as upward.

49

The actual wind that we feel and can see the effects of, is made up of a number of different types of wind. Each term in equations (3.1)–(3.3) tries to set up its own wind. So what we do is to divide the actual wind into three types.

(i) The prevailing wind: this stays the same for long periods of time so that $\frac{dU}{dt}$ is very small and we can assume that $\frac{dU}{dt} = 0$.

(ii) The tidal winds, for which $\frac{dp}{dx}$ and $\frac{dp}{dy} = 0$ since they are very small; and

(iii) The irregular winds which act over such short distances that the effect of the Coriolis force is small and $\mathscr{F}$ is the smallest term in the equation of motion so that we take $\mathscr{F} = 0$.

3.2. Prevailing winds

If you watch smoke rising from a chimney then you will see that the direction and strength of the wind is very irregular. In the upper atmosphere the wind also appears irregular and wind measurements reveal a pattern like the one shown in fig. 3.4.

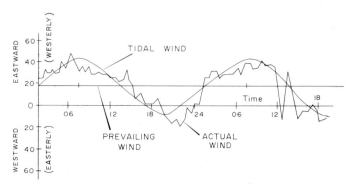

Fig. 3.4. Upper atmospheric wind measurements (in m s^{-1}) split into their prevailing and tidal components.

The wind in fig. 3.4 can be broken up into three parts. Firstly there is the prevailing wind, which is the average value of the wind taken over a couple of days. Superimposed on the prevailing wind are periodically varying tidal winds and irregular winds, both of which will be dealt with later on.

The prevailing wind stays reasonably constant over a month, changing predominantly with the seasons. Since we know that it is completely horizontal, if we can find two components of the wind then we can specify its magnitude and direction. It is usual to find

50

the components in the east–west and north–south directions. These are known as the zonal and meridional directions respectively.

The prevailing wind arises from a balance between the Coriolis force and the pressure gradient force set up by seasonal temperature changes. Mathematically,

$$\frac{1}{\rho}\frac{dp}{dx} = \mathscr{F}U_y; \quad \frac{1}{\rho}\frac{dp}{dy} = -\mathscr{F}U_x$$

where x and y represent the eastward and northward components respectively.

However we know a few more things about the nature of the pressure, p. Firstly,

$$p = \rho RT/M \text{ (ideal gas law)}$$

and secondly

$$dp/dz = -\rho g \text{ (hydrostatic equilibrium)}$$

By solving these four equations together, we can find the height variations of the prevailing wind. If we pretend that the temperature does not change with height then we get the thermal wind equations which relate the vertical changes in the wind with the horizontal changes in temperature

$$\frac{dU_x}{dz} = -\frac{g}{\mathscr{F}T}\frac{dT}{dy}; \quad \frac{dU_y}{dz} = \frac{g}{\mathscr{F}T}\frac{dT}{dx}$$

Of course the temperature does change with height so that a small correction needs to be applied to these equations.

The thermal wind equations are extremely useful to aeronomers, enabling them to deduce winds, which are difficult to measure at large altitudes, from the values of the temperature, which is easier to measure.

Figure 3.5 depicts the prevailing winds during the solstices. The upper atmosphere's general circulation is quite different from the troposphere's. The lower atmospheric circulation is dominated by a jet stream (a relatively small core of strong wind) which always blows eastward. The stratosphere has a much stronger jet stream that reverses direction from summer to winter.

The lower thermosphere has an equatorial core of westward-blowing wind. This is not due to the atmosphere's temperature distribution and it cannot be deduced from the thermal wind equations. The strong westward equatorial wind at 100 km arises from electrodynamic effects: namely, the interaction of the neutral wind with the equatorial electrojet. An electrojet is a region of fast

moving electrons and ions with speeds of about 100 m s⁻¹. The
fast moving charged particles of the equatorial electrojet collide with
the neutral particles of the air and set them moving in the same
direction with a slightly smaller speed—of about 50 m s⁻¹. Following
periods of strong solar activity another electrojet, an auroral electrojet
is also set up at 70° latitude and 100 km altitude. Because of the
random nature of the occurrence of the auroral electrojet, it can not be
considered a part of the general circulation.

The prevailing winds above 120 km are very weak, because daily
heating changes are far stronger than seasonal changes. Thermospheric winds are dealt with in Section 3.4.

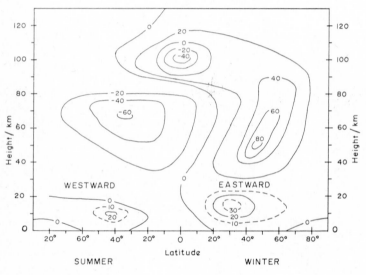

Fig. 3.5. The prevailing winds, given by the average zonal wind in m s⁻¹.

3.3. *Tides*

Every 24 hours the Sun rises and proceeds to heat the atmosphere.
This heating is accompanied by an increase in the temperature of the
sunlit half of the Earth. Supposing that the air acts like a gas heated
at constant volume the atmospheric pressure at the sunlit side is
greater and air flows from the sunlit side to the dark side of the Earth.
The Sun's heating sets up a wind. As we rotate underneath this wind
it seems to vary periodically (fig. 3.6). This is called a tide, by analogy
with the ocean's tides, though it should be remembered that the
ocean's tides are due to the gravitational effect of the Moon whereas
the atmospheric tides are due to the heating effect of the Sun.

52

A detailed mathematical analysis of tidal theory is very complicated, but we can get a simple idea of the mechanism involved by examining the most important forces producing tidal winds. These arise from the wind's acceleration and the Coriolis acceleration:

$$\frac{\mathrm{d}U_x}{\mathrm{d}t} = \mathcal{F} U_y \tag{3.4}$$

$$\frac{\mathrm{d}U_y}{\mathrm{d}t} = -\mathcal{F} U_x \tag{3.5}$$

Differentiating with respect to t, we see

$$\frac{\mathrm{d}^2U_x}{\mathrm{d}t^2} = -\mathcal{F}^2 U_x \quad \text{and} \quad \frac{\mathrm{d}^2U_y}{\mathrm{d}t^2} = -\mathcal{F}^2 U_y$$

so that two compatible solutions would be $U_x = U \sin \mathcal{F}t$ and $U_y = U \cos \mathcal{F}t$ where $\mathcal{F}$ is the Coriolis parameter $2\Omega_E \sin \phi$. These equations represent simple harmonic motion with a period $2\pi/\mathcal{F}$. Therefore, the atmosphere has a natural frequency of oscillation—a resonance frequency—corresponding to a period of 12 cosec ϕ hours.

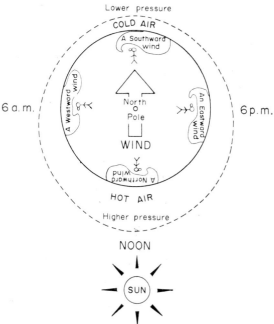

Fig. 3.6.   Why we see a tidal wind.

53

The heating effect of the Sun acts like a periodic sequence of pushes to the atmosphere. But the Sun's heating rate does not vary sinusoidally with time. It only acts during the daytime and it looks something like the curve in fig. 3.7. To evaluate the atmosphere's response (i.e. the atmosphere's ' swings ') to this type of driving force, we have to find the sinusoidal oscillations that make up the driving force of fig. 3.7.

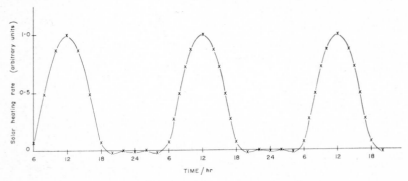

Fig. 3.7. A representation of the Sun's heating rate.

There is an important theorem in mathematics (Fourier's theorem) which says that any curve that has only one value at every point can be obtained by adding together an infinite number of perfect sinusoidal curves. The sinusoidal components which, when added together, give the curve of fig. 3.7 are shown in fig. 3.8.*

A mathematician would call these sinusoidal components the Fourier components (or harmonics) of the solar heating function, but in this particular case it is more usual to call them the tidal components. We can see that in this case we can expect a 24 hour tide, a 12 hour tide and a 6 hour tide. In general we can expect many other components as well, because *all* the waves whose periods are $24/m$ hours where $m = 1, 2, 3, 4 \ldots$ are tidal components. In practice, the only tidal components of sufficient strength to show up in the pressure or wind records are the 24, 12, 8 and 6 hour tides, with the first two being most dominant.

Since the resonant frequency varies with latitude, we would expect to find different tidal components being dominant at different latitudes and this is indeed the case. In the ionosphere long sequences of wind

* In fact to demonstrate the power of this theorem I actually calculated the sinusoidal components first and then drew fig. 3.7 by summing the curves in fig. 3.8. The little twiddles on the otherwise flat section of fig. 3.7 are there because I only took the first four sinusoidal components. The fifth, sixth, etc., components would gradually straighten the flat section when added to the curve.

measurements obtained by watching the drift of meteor trails and the drift of chemical releases from rockets show that the tidal and irregular components are larger than the prevailing wind. At Jodrell Bank, England, 53°N latitude, the diurnal (24 hour) component is small, around 5–10 m s⁻¹ and the semidiurnal (12 hour) winds are dominant, being typically 20 m s⁻¹, whereas at Adelaide, South Australia, 35°S, the diurnal wind of 30 m s⁻¹ slightly exceeds the semidiurnal wind.

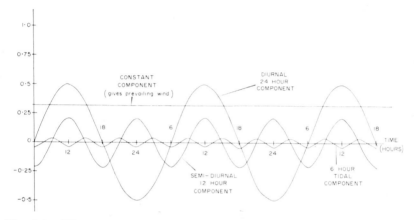

Fig. 3.8. The Fourier components whose sum gives the solar heating rate.

The speeds of the tidal winds near the ground are exceedingly small. The reason for this is that the energy per unit volume of tides, $\frac{1}{2}\rho U^2$, must be conserved (i.e. stay constant at all heights). But we know that ρ decreases exponentially with height

$$\rho = \rho_0 \exp\left(-z/H\right)$$

so

$$U = \sqrt{(U_x{}^2 + U_y{}^2)} = U_0 \exp\left(z/2H\right) \tag{3.6}$$

and the tidal wind-speed increases in magnitude as one ascends.

The tidal winds at the ground, U_0, are exceedingly small. At the ground one can best observe the atmospheric tides by watching the changes on a barometer. The tides at the ground are not only weaker, but their nature is different to the upper atmospheric tides. In the upper atmosphere the diurnal tide is dominant at low latitudes and the semidiurnal tide dominates at high latitudes. At the ground the semidiurnal tide is dominant everywhere. This is because the thermal structure of the ozone layer and the lower atmosphere affect the resonance properties in such a way as to enhance the semidiurnal tide.

55

3.4. *Thermospheric winds*

The only systematic way of studying neutral atmospheric winds above 200 km is to watch the changes in the orbits of artificial satellites. From these, the air density can be deduced, then the air pressure and then finally the winds. The results obtained by this method indicate that fig. 3.9 is a good picture of the thermospheric winds. There is a characteristic bulge of the thermosphere at 1400 hours and the winds blow away from this bulge on all sides. The isotherms (for constant temperature) and the isobars (for constant pressure), which are depicted on fig. 3.9, coincide with one another in the thermosphere. Thus the winds in the thermosphere are tidal winds with periods of 24 hours.

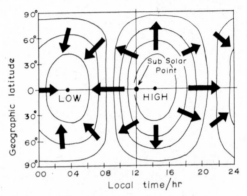

Fig. 3.9.   The thermospheric wind system.

The thermosphere has a very high thermal conductivity and a very high kinematic viscosity. The high thermal conductivity means that heat supplied at one height is quickly transported to all other heights in the thermosphere which thus has a constant temperature throughout. Since the principal heat input to the thermosphere comes from the solar XUV radiation, the high thermal conductivity means that at night, when heat is not being deposited, there is a considerable temperature change. This large difference between day and night temperatures leads to the diurnal bulge.

I have said that the thermosphere has a high kinematic viscosity. Let me explain this further. There are two coefficients of viscosity in common use. The coefficient of dynamic viscosity, η, of a fluid is defined by the relation

$$F = \eta A \frac{\mathrm{d}U}{\mathrm{d}z}$$

where F is the viscous force parallel to the direction of motion U, exerted on area A when the velocity gradient at right angles to the area is $\mathrm{d}U/\mathrm{d}z$.

In a gas, η increases with temperature, and the variation of η with temperature can be calculated using the kinetic theory. The temperature in the thermosphere is much higher than elsewhere in the atmosphere, so η is correspondingly higher; η provides a measure of the viscous force.

It is convenient in fluid dynamics to define the coefficient of kinematic viscosity, μ, where

$$\mu = \eta / \rho$$

so that μ gives a measure of the *accelerations* required to maintain the viscous forces. When we study air motions we are primarily concerned with velocities and accelerations so that it is the value of the coefficient of kinematic viscosity that we need. In the thermosphere, η is high and the density ρ is low so that μ has a large value which increases exponentially in value upwards as the density decreases.

Viscosity is an effect due to molecular friction. In the thermosphere there is another kind of friction, called ion drag, which will tend to slow down the air molecules and reduce the wind speed. Ion drag occurs because the heavy ions that comprise the ionosphere are restricted in motion by the Earth's magnetic field. So a wind, which is a movement of the neutral (un-ionized) particles of the atmosphere, results in the neutral particles continuously colliding with the almost stationary ions.

The thermospheric wind is then a balance between the pressure-gradient forces set up by the Sun's heating effect and the frictional forces caused by viscosity and ion drag. The frictional forces prevent any strong gradients being set up in the wind system so that the wind velocities at any one time are the same at all heights above 200 km. We can represent all the winds in the thermosphere from 200 km up to 600 km quite well by one diagram (fig. 3.9).

The results deduced from observations of satellite orbits indicate that when the thermospheric winds are averaged over one day then the thermosphere rotates 1·3 times as fast as the Earth. This phenomenon is called atmospheric super-rotation and it is equivalent to a prevailing wind of about $0\cdot3 R_E \Omega_E \cos \phi$, where R_E is the radius of the Earth and Ω_E its angular velocity. The reason for this super-rotation is not yet completely clear. The most plausible theory suggests that electric fields are produced during the night which enable the ions to move. This reduces the ion drag at night and means that the air moves slightly faster at night than during the day, so that when one takes the mean value over 24 hours there is a slight prevailing wind.

3.5. *Irregular winds*

The motions depicted in fig. 3.4 reveal a scattering of values about the smooth oscillation of the tidal winds. This scatter evidently results from a superimposed irregular motion of the atmosphere. Observations of the irregular wind show that its strength increases with height. In the ionosphere the irregular, fluctuating, wind is in general stronger than either the prevailing wind or the tidal winds.

It was at first believed that this irregular wind was a result of atmospheric turbulence. The discovery of the turbopause indicated that this could not be so, since the irregular wind is strongest in just those regions where we would expect no turbulence. Eventually, it was realized that the irregular wind could be described in terms of a particular type of wave motion of the atmosphere. At any one time there are a large number of such waves present with various wavelengths and periods, so that when they all combine to give the fluctuating wind pattern it can appear very irregular.

The atmospheric waves responsible for the irregular wind are called gravity waves, because they are set up by the competing effect of buoyancy forces and gravity when the hydrostatic equilibrium is perturbed. Imagine that you start with an atmosphere in hydrostatic

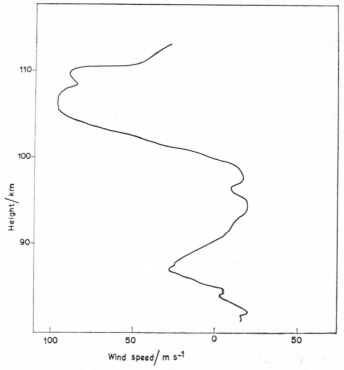

Fig. 3.10. A long-lasting meteor trail distorted by the irregular wind. The wind can be seen as a wave whose amplitude grows with height.

equilibrium and then move a packet of air upwards. Because the density of the air decreases going upwards this packet will now be heavier than the surrounding air and it will sink. In the absence of appreciable friction it will overshoot its equilibrium position. Since we have seen that atmospheric friction is only important in the lowest 1 km of the atmosphere and in the thermosphere, this overshooting is very likely to happen.

Once the packet of air has overshot below its equilibrium position, it will be lighter than the surrounding air and it will rise, overshoot the equilibrium position and so continue to oscillate. This sets up the gravity wave.

One method of disturbing the atmosphere is by solar heating, and in fact all the atmospheric tides (except the diurnal, 24 hour tide which is a very special case) are also gravity waves. However, there are more gravity wave modes than tidal modes because many other effects can set up gravity waves; the wind blowing over mountain ranges, earthquakes, nuclear explosions and fluctuations in the strong wind systems of the lower atmosphere. Gravity waves are very like atmospheric tides and have many properties in common. Most significantly, the amplitudes of both tides and gravity waves increase with altitude (equation 3.6) and this is the reason for the strength of the irregular wind in the ionosphere.

The discovery that the upper atmospheric winds could be described in terms of these wave motions greatly enriched our understanding of aeronomy. It is very difficult to make accurate predictions or good mathematical models of turbulence, but waves are well understood and equations can be found to describe them. Thus, once the winds can be mathematically described then one can start on the complex problem of determining the interaction of the ionosphere with the wind, a problem that is still being actively worked on.

3.6. *The dynamo region*

A properly mounted magnetic compass sets with its axis in line with the horizontal component of the Earth's magnetic field. A detailed study of a magnetic compass fixed at one place shows small movements of the compass needle about its equilibrium position, indicating changes in the direction of the Earth's field. Often these movements are regular and periodic, with the same variations occurring at the same time of day. Days with regular magnetic variations are known as magnetically quiet days. On other days there are large unpredictable variations in the magnetic field. These days are known as magnetically disturbed days.

Magnetically disturbed days are related to solar activity, but the periodic variations evident on magnetically quiet days are related to the motions of the ionosphere. The periodic fluctuations recorded on delicate magnetic instruments are due to the tidal winds in the ionospheric E region! How does this come about?

Firstly we must remember that in the E region when a wind blows across the magnetic field lines, then the electrons can move with the wind but the heavier ions are restricted by the magnetic field. In other words the wind sets up a 'conventional current' in the opposite direction to which the wind blows. This is very much like the situation in a piece of copper wire connected to a battery. The potential gradient along the wire drives the electrons but the positive copper ions do not move. By convention, the current is taken as flowing in the direction opposite to the electrons' motion.

Elementary electrical experiments show that an electric current has a magnetic field associated with it that is set up by the current. A long straight current-carrying wire has a pattern of circular magnetic flux-lines looping around the wire whose magnitudes and directions are given by the Biot–Savart law. Thus the moving electrons behave like an electric current in a wire and set up an extra magnetic field which affects compass needles at the ground. As the wind reverses, so does the direction of this extra magnetic field.

The first explanations of the daily magnetic variations ascribed them to the action of an atmospheric dynamo. In a typical dynamo, an electric current flows in a conductor while it is moving across the flux lines of a magnetic field, which is provided by a stationary magnet system. In the upper atmosphere the Earth's magnetic field corresponds to the magnet and the electron-stream to the conductor, while the tidal winds provide the motion.

The strength of the dynamo effect depends on the conductivity of the conductor. The conductivity, in turn, depends on the number of electrons, N, since the current density $\mathbf{J}$ (A m^{-2}) is given by

$$\mathbf{J} = \sigma\mathbf{E} = Ne\mathbf{v}$$

where σ is the ionospheric conductivity, $\mathbf{E}$ is the electric field set up by the wind which can be thought of as providing the energy to move the electrons, of charge e, at a drift velocity $\mathbf{v}$. The dynamo effect is confined to a narrow height range centred on 100 km altitude and this is called the dynamo region. It corresponds to the region of the ionosphere with the highest conductivity.

On this theory, one can work out the current system needed in the dynamo region in order to produce the observed daily variations in the magnetic field (fig. 3.11). As the Earth rotates underneath this current system, known as the Sq current system (S = solar, q = quiet), the local magnetic field changes. The currents flowing in the atmospheric dynamo on the day side are greater than those on the night side because the electron density, and hence the ionospheric conductivity, is much greater during the day.

60

The arrows on fig. 3.11 indicate the directions of current flow and the lines are drawn such that between each pair of adjacent lines a current of 10 000 A flows. There are four current systems, two to the north and two to the south of the Equator, each flowing around a focus. During the equinoxes the current system is symmetrical about the Equator (as drawn), but this symmetry is lost at other times of the year, and the current in the summer hemisphere is increased. The total current flow in the day-circuit in the northern hemisphere is 89 000 A in June but is reduced to 65 000 A at the equinoxes.

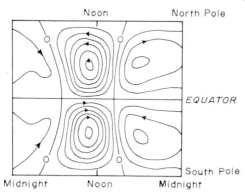

Fig. 3.11. The Sq current system in the dynamo region.

Quiet magnetic variations provided the first means of determining upper atmospheric winds, currents and electric fields. Further work revealed that the moon's gravitational field also influenced the atmosphere, producing the very much weaker Lq current system (L = lunar, q = quiet). Nowadays more sophisticated methods, such as the barium release technique, are being used to study the winds and fields so that the chief attention is shifting from the quiet magnetic variations to the disturbed magnetic variations.

Further reading:
Beer, Tom, 1972. Atmospheric waves and the ionosphere, *Contemporary Physics*, **13**, 247–271.
Groves, G. V., 1973. The structure of the atmosphere up to 150 kilometre, *Contemporary Physics*, **14**, 1–24.
Hines, C. O., 1963. The upper atmosphere in motion, *Quarterly Journal of the Royal Meteorological Society*, **89**, 1–42.
Newell, Reginald E., 1964. The circulation of the upper atmosphere, *Scientific American*, **210** (3), 62–74.

Once again, these are more detailed expositions at about the same level as this chapter. Hines' and Beer's articles are slightly more difficult than the other two. Reference books on these topics are:
Beer, Tom, 1974. *Atmospheric Waves.* (London: Adam Hilger.)
Eckart, Carl, 1960. *Hydrodynamics of Oceans and Atmospheres.* (Oxford: Pergamon Press.)

61

CHAPTER 4

radio waves and telecommunications

4.1. *Introduction*

RADIO waves are electromagnetic waves of frequencies below 3000 MHz, which corresponds to a wavelength of about 10 cm. Waves shorter than this (i.e. at higher frequencies) are known as microwaves. There is really no clear-cut delineation between the microwave region and the radio wave region, though wavelengths of order millimetres and centimetres are usually called microwaves; while radio wavelengths are measured in metres (Table 4.1).

Microwaves are often used for telecommunications over short distances, for high frequency radio waves and microwaves pass right through the ionosphere (see fig. 1.5, p. 13). Electromagnetic waves 'travel in straight lines', but the Earth is curved. Thus, microwaves are unsuitable for long distance communication since they cannot be reflected around the horizon unless relay satellites are used. In order to communicate by radio over long distances without going to the expense of using satellites, we must use radio waves that will be reflected by the ionosphere.

We know that in free space and in air all electromagnetic waves move with a speed $c = 1/\sqrt{(\mu_0 \epsilon_0)}$, the speed of light in vacuum; ϵ_0 is the permittivity of a vacuum and μ_0 is the permeability of a vacuum. When radio waves move through the ionosphere however, the speed will change to an extent depending on the frequency of the wave. And, when a radio wave is reflected back along its own path, there must be an instant at which the velocity has dropped to zero!

Frequency, f, and wavelength, λ, in a given medium, of the wave are related by

$$f\lambda = v,$$

where v is the velocity/speed in that medium and we can see that the wavelength will change as the wave passes through the ionosphere.

An electromagnetic wave travels with an electric field vector and a magnetic field vector which oscillate in planes perpendicular to each other and perpendicular to the direction of travel. Figure 4.1 represents a plane-polarized wave—the plane of polarization being chosen as that of the electric vector.

62

Name	Frequency	Wavelength	Use
Microwave	300 GHz–3 GHz	0·1 cm–10 cm	Satellites, Radar, Microwave links
Ultra high frequency (u.h.f.)	3000 MHz–300 MHz	10 cm–1 cm	F.M. radio, T.V.
Very high frequency (v.h.f.)	300 MHz–30 MHz	1 m–10 m	T.V., Police, Taxis
High frequency (h.f.)	30 MHz–3 MHz	10 m–100 m	Short wave radio
Medium frequency (m.f.)	3000 kHz–300 kHz	100 m–1 km	Local broadcasting, Ship and aircraft radio beacons
Low frequency (l.f.)	300 kHz–30 kHz	1 km–10 km	Long range navigation aids
Very low frequency (v.l.f.)	30 kHz–3 kHz	10 km–100 km	Submarine communication, Global navigation systems

Table 4.1. The radio wave spectrum.

In a plasma there is an interaction between the electrons and an electromagnetic wave. The electrons in the plasma oscillate under the electric-vector force which varies sinusoidally with time.

We can imagine free electrons in a plasma to be bound to much heavier ions as if they were attached to each other by a weak simple spring. After the electric field of the electromagnetic wave has separated a free electron from a nearby free ion, the electric field between the electron and ion acts like the restoring force of a spring. Electrons are set in motion at precisely the same frequency as that of the incident wave, a frequency which may differ from the 'natural frequency' of the electrons. The 'natural frequency' is that frequency with which the electrons would oscillate (under their 'weak springs') if after being disturbed, they were left free of an external driving force. The natural frequency of electron oscillation is called the plasma frequency.

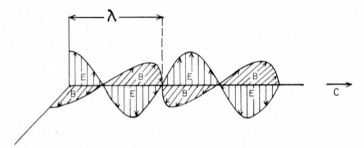

Fig. 4.1. Representation of the amplitudes and directions of the electric and magnetic fields of a linearly polarized electromagnetic wave.

As a consequence of their continuous acceleration in the electromagnetic wave, the oscillating electrons themselves act as generators of electromagnetic radiation. In short, when radiation is incident upon an electric charge, the charge re-radiates the radiation. The nature of the re-radiation—whether the electromagnetic wave is reflected, refracted or scattered depends on the nature of the medium.

4.2. *The plasma frequency and reflection*

The plasma frequency is the natural oscillation frequency of electrons in a plasma. It is easy to derive an expression for the plasma frequency by using Gauss's law—which says that the normal component of electric field $\mathbf{E}$ through a closed surface of area $\mathrm{d}\mathscr{A}$ is given by the charges, Q, within the volume bounded by the surface, through the relation

$$\int \mathbf{E}_n \cdot \mathrm{d}\mathscr{A} = \frac{Q}{\epsilon_0}$$

64

Let us apply Gauss's law to the situation in fig. 4.2. We have N electrons per cubic metre separated by a distance x from N ions per cubic metre. There is going to be an electric field set up that will attempt to restore the charges to their original position. If we integrate the electric field over a cylinder, which encloses the ions at one end, then we can see that

$$\mathbf{E}\,d\mathscr{A} = \frac{N|e|x d\mathscr{A}}{\epsilon_0}$$

since the total charge on the ions $Q = N|e|x d\mathscr{A}$ where $e = -1\cdot6 \times 10^{-19}$ C is the charge on the electron.

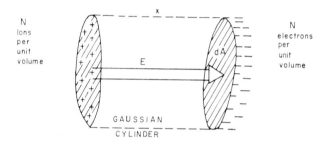

Fig. 4.2. Electric field set up when charges are separated.

The restoring force on the electrons acts in the opposite direction to $\mathbf{E}$ and it is given by

$$F = m\frac{d^2x}{dt^2} = -|e|\mathbf{E}$$

so that when we substitute the expression for $\mathbf{E}$ we find that

$$\frac{d^2x}{dt^2} + \frac{Ne^2}{\epsilon_0 m_e}x = 0$$

where m_e is the mass of the electron. This equation tells us that the electrons undergo simple harmonic motion about the ions. The angular frequency of this motion which we shall denote by ω_p is given by

$$\omega_p{}^2 = \frac{Ne^2}{\epsilon_0 m_e}$$

so that the plasma frequency is

$$f_p{}^2 = \frac{Ne^2}{4\pi^2\epsilon_0 m_e}.$$

65

The existence of a natural resonance frequency should warn us to look out for two physical effects:

(i) the velocity of the wave will be different at different frequencies and

(ii) the natural resonance frequency is liable to act as a cut-off frequency and prevent waves of frequency lower than this from propagating through the medium.

If we have an electromagnetic wave propagating through a collision-less magnetic-field-free plasma then the refractive index, n, of the plasma depends on the frequency, f, of the wave. It is given by

$$n^2 = 1 - \frac{f_p{}^2}{f^2} = 1 - \frac{Ne^2}{4\pi^2\epsilon_0 m_e f^2} \qquad (4.1)$$

The wave will be reflected when $n^2 \leqslant 0$, and this occurs if the wave frequency drops below the plasma frequency.

We can also write the refractive index in terms of the wavelength, λ, of the electromagnetic wave within the plasma as

$$n = \frac{c}{f\lambda} = \frac{c}{v}$$

this indicates that the velocity of the wave is going to change as the frequency f changes, and it is going to increase as f decreases until it becomes infinite when reflection takes place. The physical reason for this is depicted in fig. 4.3, where we show the wavefronts as the electromagnetic wave impinges on a plasma. Outside the plasma the wavefronts advance with a velocity v, but as soon as they reach the plasma the wavefronts have to 'turn around' in order to be reflected. Since the reflection is taking place at one point the wavefront has to

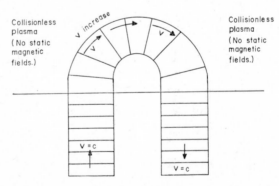

Fig. 4.3. The phase velocity, v, of an electromagnetic wave increases when the wave is reflected.

turn around instantaneously, or in other words the velocity of the wavefront has to be infinite.

In Section 4.1 I said that when a wave is reflected its velocity is going to be zero. Now I claim that its velocity is going to be infinite. How can both statements be true? To understand this we must remember a point that is always important with any kind of wave motion. A steady uninterrupted wave with constant strength and fixed frequency would be no use in an experiment designed to find the level of reflection since it would simply produce a constant unvarying response in the receiver from which nothing could be deduced. To make it useful in carrying signals, the wave must be transmitted in packets (groups or pulses), whose arrival at the receiver can be timed.

If the speed of a wave varies with its frequency, as it does in a plasma like the ionosphere, then the speed of the wavepacket is not the same as the speed of the waves comprising the wavepacket. This is shown in fig. 4.4. The same effect can be demonstrated by dropping

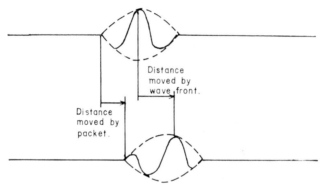

Fig. 4.4. The velocity of the wavefronts (the phase velocity) does not always equal the velocity of the wavepackets (the group velocity). Energy travels with the wavepackets.

a stone into a still lake. This produces a wavepacket composed of two or three crests. As the wavepacket moves along the surface of the water, away from the spot where the stone was dropped in, the leading trough is gradually overtaken by the crest behind it. Thus the trough moves out of the packet which now has a crest leading it. This crest also moves faster than the packet and soon disappears to be replaced by a trough, and so on. Electromagnetic wave packets behave in the same way when they move through an ionized medium. The waves comprising the wavepacket move at a velocity (called the *phase velocity*) which is faster than the velocity of the packet itself (*the group velocity*). When reflection takes place, the packet slows down, stops, and returns back the way it came. At the same time the wavefronts within the packet are speeding up (fig. 4.3). At reflection the phase velocity is infinite and the group velocity is zero. The variation of these two velocities as the wave frequency changes is shown in fig. 4.5. For extremely high frequency waves (such as light with a frequency of the order of 10^{14} Hz, greatly exceeding the maximum ionospheric plasma frequency of 10^7 Hz) the refractive index stays at unity; both the wavepackets and the wavefronts move at c, the speed of light, and so the light waves are unaffected by the ionosphere. On the other hand, electrons within a metal have their own very high plasma frequency which is so high that it interacts with light. Metal mirrors reflect light; the ionosphere reflects radio waves. The same phenomenon occurs in each case, but different values of the plasma frequency are responsible for the different reflection frequencies.

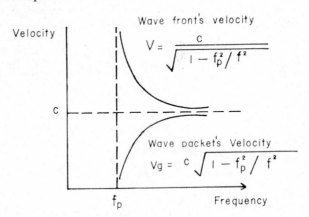

Fig. 4.5.   The phase velocity (v) and the group velocity (v_g), for an electromagnetic wave propagating through a plasma in the absence of a static magnetic field and of collisions.

4.3. The gyrofrequency and wave splitting

The ionosphere cannot really be thought of as a magnetic-field-free plasma because the Earth's magnetic field permeates all the ionosphere. The strength of the Earth's magnetic field decreases as one moves away from the Earth, and there are also slight variations at the same altitude at different locations. Values of the magnetic flux density at the F region peak range between 0.3×10^{-4} T and 0.5×10^{-4} T. The electron gyrofrequency for a field of 0.5×10^{-4} T is 1.4 MHz, which is well within the normal operating frequency of ionosondes (see Section 1.5, page 17). There is thus going to be a two stage interaction; first between the radio wave and the electrons in the

68

ionosphere and then between the electrons and the terrestrial magnetic field. This interaction produces two radio waves of different polarizations which travel with different velocities through the ionosphere. These two radio waves appear as two separate traces on an ionogram. These traces can be seen in fig. 4.6 which is a reproduction of an ionogram taken at Legon, Ghana. The splitting is very prominent on the F region trace but can sometimes also be seen on E region reflections.

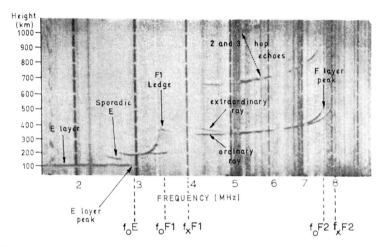

Fig. 4.6. Ionogram from Legon, near Accra, Ghana taken at noon on April 14, 1965.

We have seen that in a magnetic-field-free plasma the radio wave is reflected when

$$n^2 = 1 - X = 0$$

where X stands for f_p^2/f^2 (notice that X is a ratio of squares). When there is a magnetic field present then there are two reflection criteria:

$$X = 1 \text{ for one trace,}$$

$$\text{and } \begin{cases} X = 1 - Y \text{ if } Y < 1 \\ X = 1 + Y \text{ if } Y \geqslant 1 \end{cases}$$

for the other trace, where, in the standard ionospheric notation,

$$Y = f_B/f = eB/(2\pi mf)$$

(notice that this is *not* a ratio of squares). One wave is totally unaffected by the magnetic field whereas the other has its reflection frequency seriously modified by the presence of the magnetic field.

69

The wave that is unaffected, and reflected when $X=1$, is called the ordinary wave. The other wave is called the extraordinary wave.

We can use the ionogram of fig. 4.6 to compute Y, and thus to find B, at the ionospheric peaks. For example, at the F2 region peak, $X=1$ implies that the plasma frequency f_p is equal to the ordinary wave reflection frequency, f_0 F2, which is 7·4 MHz since the frequency scale in fig. 4.6 is logarithmic. So we can see that

$$\frac{(f_0\,\mathrm{F2})^2}{(f_x\,\mathrm{F2})^2} = \left[1 - \frac{f_\mathrm{B}}{f_x\,\mathrm{F2}}\right]$$

and by applying the binomial theorem this can be put in the convenient form

$$f_{0c} \approx f_{xc} - \tfrac{1}{2}f_\mathrm{B}$$

where the subscript c indicates that the frequencies are measured at the critical frequencies corresponding to the layer peaks. Since f_x F2 in fig. 4.6 corresponds to 8·0 MHz we obtain a gyrofrequency of 1·2 MHz at the F2 region peak in this case.

Characteristic waves

The ordinary and extraordinary waves make up the characteristic waves of the ionosphere. What is a characteristic wave? It is a wave which does not change its polarization when it travels through the ionosphere. There are two, and only two, characteristic waves in the ionosphere.

The polarization of the characteristic wave depends on the angle, θ, that the electromagnetic wave makes with the magnetic field, provided that the wave is not near its critical frequency. When θ is 0° or 180° the electromagnetic wave travels parallel to the magnetic field and this is known as longitudinal propagation—an example would be a radio wave propagated vertically upwards at the magnetic pole. When θ is 90° the electromagnetic wave travels perpendicular to the magnetic field and this is known as transverse propagation—such as occurs when a radio wave is propagated vertically upwards at the magnetic equator.

For longitudinal propagation the characteristic waves are circularly polarized. The reason for this follows directly from the fact that electrons rotate in clockwise circles around magnetic field lines when viewed by an observer looking in the same direction as the magnetic field. Electromagnetic waves which are circularly polarized have a transverse* electric field vector which rotates in a circle as the electromagnetic wave progresses. This rotating electric field interacts with the electrons. When $Y>1$ and $\theta=0°$ then an anticlockwise

---

* In effect, perpendicular to the direction of motion of the wave—in this case this is also perpendicular to the Earth's magnetic field.

rotation of the electric field is not affected by the electrons. However, a clockwise rotating **E** is 'speeded up' by the electrons and this faster wave is the extraordinary wave. In this case the ordinary wave is left-hand circularly polarized and the extraordinary wave is right-hand circularly polarized. (The handedness is defined in relation to someone looking along the direction of wave motion.)

During transverse propagation, $\theta = 90°$, the characteristic waves are linearly polarized. We should recall that electrons are free to slide along magnetic field lines but are extremely resistant to motion across magnetic field lines. Thus the transverse radio waves with its electric field vector parallel to the magnetic field must be the ordinary wave—and it is the characteristic wave because it simulates the electron's motion. The extraordinary wave is the linearly polarized wave whose electric field vector is perpendicular to the magnetic field.

Faraday rotation

Now that we have found out what the characteristic waves in the ionosphere are, we can discuss what happens to a wave that is not a characteristic wave when it propagates through the ionosphere. Imagine a linearly polarized radio wave propagating parallel to the Earth's magnetic field (fig. 4.7). (Remember that a linearly polarized wave is the characteristic wave only if it propagates perpendicular to the magnetic field.) As soon as this wave enters the ionosphere its plane of polarization starts to rotate. This is known as Faraday rotation.

To understand Faraday rotation, one must first realize that any linearly polarized wave can be thought of as a combination of two circularly polarized waves in phase, but rotating in opposite directions. This is depicted in fig. 4.8. The two circularly polarized waves—whose vector sum produces the linearly polarized wave—are the

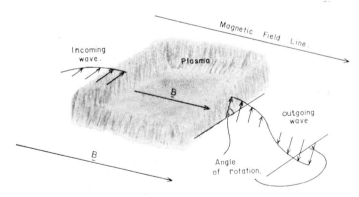

Fig. 4.7. Faraday rotation of a linearly polarized wave during longitudinal propagation (the oscillating magnetic field of the wave is not shown).

71

characteristic waves in this case. Their polarization does not change but one of them moves faster through the ionosphere than the other one. When $Y < 1$, the faster wave is the extraordinary wave.

As the linearly polarized wave moves through the ionosphere, the two characteristic waves move out of phase. This rotates the plane

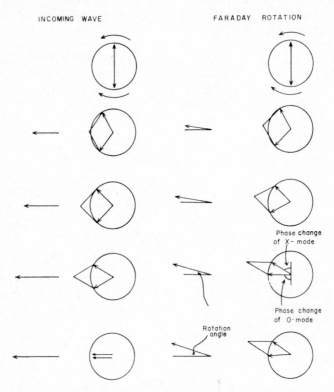

INCOMING WAVE   FARADAY   ROTATION

Phase change
of X - mode

Phase change
of O-mode

Rotation
angle

Fig. 4.8 (a). A linearly polarized wave is the vector sum of two circularly polarized waves of half the amplitude rotating in opposite directions. If the two circularly polarized waves are not in phase, i.e. their speeds do not match, then the plane of the linear wave rotates. Note that the phase change of the faster wave (the X mode in this case) is the lesser.

of polarization of the linear wave, as shown in fig. 4.8. As soon as the waves emerge from the ionosphere, both characteristic waves move at exactly the same speed, which is the speed of light, so that the plane of the linear wave upon emerging from the ionosphere ceases to rotate.

This is fortunate because it means that if we examine the Faraday rotation angle of a radio wave that has reached the ground then we know that it had the same rotation angle on emerging from the

72

ionosphere. Provided we know the initial direction of the wave's polarization, we can extract useful information about the ionosphere.

There are two major ways of using Faraday rotation to study the ionosphere. One method transmits a signal of known polarization from the ground, reflects it from the Moon or an artificial satellite, and measures the resulting rotation angle. Since the wave goes through the ionosphere twice, the angle will be double that produced

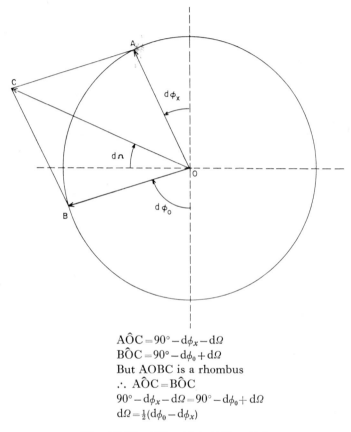

$$A\hat{O}C = 90° - d\phi_x - d\Omega$$
$$B\hat{O}C = 90° - d\phi_0 + d\Omega$$
But AOBC is a rhombus
$$\therefore \ A\hat{O}C = B\hat{O}C$$
$$90° - d\phi_x - d\Omega = 90° - d\phi_0 + d\Omega$$
$$d\Omega = \tfrac{1}{2}(d\phi_0 - d\phi_x)$$

Fig. 4.8 (b).   Why $d\Omega$ is $\tfrac{1}{2}(d\phi_0 - d\phi_x)$.

by a single journey. The second method is to examine the Faraday rotation suffered by radio waves transmitted from a satellite. This is easier than transmitting your own signals and provided that someone else pays for the satellite it is a much cheaper method as well. Obligingly enough, there are various communications satellites placed so as to remain at a fixed position above an observer on the Earth, and the organizations which launched the satellites publish lists specifying the polarization of the signals transmitted.

When the Faraday rotation angle has been measured, it is possible—by using the mathematics of Section 4.5—to find the total electron content in a vertical slab of ionosphere. If one divides the total electron content by the value of the electron density at the F2 region peak then the resulting distance is known as the ionospheric slab thickness. The slab thickness provides a rough measure of the ionospheric temperature.

Faraday rotation occurs when any electromagnetic wave passes through any plasma lying within a magnetic field. For example, linearly polarized light passing through water will suffer a small rotation of the plane of polarization when the water lies within a strong magnetic field and the light moves parallel to the field. The reason that water acts like a plasma is that the light is propagated through the water by successively exciting each electron. The first electron that the light hits absorbs the light and then re-radiates it. The next electron absorbs the re-radiated light and re-emits it, and so on. For solids and liquids the Faraday rotation is extremely small unless the material is ferromagnetic. Admittedly the Faraday rotation of the ionosphere, when expressed in terms of degrees per metre per tesla (the Verdet constant) is only about 30, as compared to 200 for water, but the large vertical extent of the ionosphere makes this a far from negligible effect.

4.4. Collisions and absorption

We have just seen that an electromagnetic wave propagates through any medium by continually being absorbed and re-radiated by the electrons in the path of the ray. Electrons are set in motion by the electric vector of the electromagnetic wave, and will vibrate at the same frequency as the wave. If the electron suffers any collisions during this vibration then its ability to re-radiate the wave will be seriously impaired, and the wave will become absorbed. In other words, part or all of the wave energy may be transferred to the random motion of the neutral particles, increasing the temperature slightly.

Electrons collide with both ions and neutral particles and in addition will sometimes collide with other electrons. Electron–electron collisions are rare because of the repulsive Coulomb forces arising from their like charge. Electron–ion collisions are also not very important when we contrast them to electron–neutral collisions because in the lower ionosphere there are so many more neutrals than ions that in the D and lower E regions the electron–neutral collision frequency is around two orders of magnitude larger than the electron–ion collision frequency anywhere in the ionosphere. (Check

74

this with Table 1.2.) Since the number of neutral particles decreases exponentially with height, the number of collisions will decrease with height. Collisions are of great importance in the D region at the base of the ionosphere. Absorption due to collisions in the D region determines the lower limit on the frequency of short (h.f.) radio waves that can be used.

The refractive index for a radio wave incident upon a magnetic-field-free plasma undergoing collisions is given by

$$n^2 = 1 - \frac{X}{1+Z^2} - i\frac{XZ}{1+Z^2} \tag{4.2}$$

where $Z = \nu/\omega$ is the ratio of the collision frequency ν to the radio wave's angular frequency ω and i is the square root of minus one.

The refractive index is a complex number! Let us pause for a moment to consider the meaning of this. The equation for one component, say the x component of the electric field vector of a wave travelling in the z direction is

$$E_x = E_0 \cos\left(\omega t - \frac{\omega}{c}nz\right)$$

Since we know that

$$\exp(i\Phi) = \cos\Phi + i\sin\Phi$$

we can write

$$E_x = E_0 \operatorname{Re}\left\{\exp\left[i\left(\omega t - \frac{\omega}{c}nz\right)\right]\right\}$$

where Re $\{\}$ means to take the real part of the expression inside the braces. If

$$n = \mu - i\chi$$

then μ stands for the real part of the refractive index and $-\chi$ is the imaginary part. In this case we can see that

$$E_x = E_0 \exp\left(-\frac{\omega}{c}\chi z\right)\operatorname{Re}\left\{\exp\left[i\left(\omega t - \frac{\omega}{c}\mu z\right)\right]\right\} \tag{4.3}$$

Since $\exp\left(-\frac{\omega}{c}\chi z\right)$ is a real number already, we were justified in bringing it outside the Re $\{\}$ operator. This expression now tells us that E_x is still wavelike but when χ is not zero then the amplitude decreases exponentially as z increases. The quantity $(\omega/c)\chi$ is a measure of the decay of amplitude per unit distance and is called the absorption coefficient.

75

By manipulating equation 4.2 we get the absorption coefficient*

$$\omega\chi/c = \frac{\omega}{c}\frac{1}{2\mu}\frac{XZ}{1+Z^2} = \frac{e^2}{2\epsilon_0 m_e c}\frac{1}{\mu}\frac{N\nu}{\omega^2+\nu^2}$$

This equation enables us to distinguish between two types of absorption, namely:

Non-deviative absorption, which is the normal form of absorption for a wave travelling through the D region of the ionosphere. It occurs when μ is near unity and when there are a large number of collisions so that the product $N\nu$ is large.

Deviative absorption occurs near the level of reflection, and at any other time when there is marked bending of the ray, that is, when μ tends to zero.

It is the D region that is responsible for the absorption of radio waves. The D region disappears at night, non-deviative absorption ceases, and all radio reception which relies on reflection from the ionosphere improves dramatically in signal strength. You will be able to listen to transmissions from a much greater distance at night than you can during the day. Short wave radio reception is improved and on the medium wave band you may be able to pick up broadcasts from other cities or towns.

4.5. *The refractive index*

So far we have met expressions for the refractive index of a radio wave in a collisionless magnetic-field-free plasma (equation 4.1) and in the case of collisions (equation 4.2). The equation for the refractive index when both collisions and magnetic fields are present depends on the angle θ between the direction of the radio wave and the magnetic field. The equation giving the refractive index is called the Appleton–Hartree equation, and it is

$$\begin{aligned} n^2 = 1 - [2X(1-X-iZ)]/ \\ [2(1-iZ)(1-X-iZ) - Y^2\sin^2\theta \\ \pm \sqrt{(Y^4\sin^4\theta + 4Y^2(1-X-iZ)^2\cos^2\theta)}] \end{aligned} \quad (4.4)$$

where, to recapitulate,

$$X = f_p^2/f^2 = Ne^2/(4\pi^2\epsilon_0 m_e f^2)$$
$$Y = f_B/f = eB/(2\pi m_e f)$$
$$Z = \nu/\omega = \nu/(2\pi f)$$

It is easy to see that equations 4.1 and 4.2 are special cases of the Appleton–Hartree equation with $Y=0$.

* Use $n^2 = \mu^2 - \chi^2 - 2i\mu\chi$ and equate the imaginary part of this with the imaginary part of eqn. (4.2).

The two roots of the denominator show that there are two characteristic waves, and the reflection conditions can be found by setting the real part of n equal to zero.

Let us try to examine the Faraday rotation of a wave propagating longitudinally ($\theta = 0°$) by using the Appleton–Hartree equation. Typical frequencies of satellite signals passing through the ionosphere are around 130 MHz. If we examine Table 1.2 we see that the collision frequency in the lowest part of the ionosphere is only about 10^6 s^{-1}, so that $Z \ll 1$ and we can neglect collisions. In this case

$$n^2 = 1 - \frac{X}{1 \pm Y}$$

At 130 MHz, $X \ll 1$ and $Y \ll 1$ as well so that by using the binomial theorem

$$n \approx 1 + \frac{X}{2} \pm \frac{XY}{2}$$

Each component of the wave undergoes a phase change dΦ as it moves through the ionosphere. If the wave moves through a distance ds then we can see from equation 4.3 that its phase changes by $\frac{\omega}{c}\mu\,\mathrm{d}s$. Since the extraordinary refractive index n_x does not equal the ordinary refractive index n_0 the two phase changes are not equal. If we now look at fig. 4.8 we can see that the phase change of each characteristic wave corresponds to the angle between the circularly polarized wave vector and the vertical because the vertical represents the position of the wave vector when it entered the ionosphere.

The Faraday rotation angle dΩ is then (see fig. 4.8)

$$\mathrm{d}\Omega = \tfrac{1}{2}(\mathrm{d}\Phi_0 - \mathrm{d}\Phi_x)$$

$$= \tfrac{1}{2}\frac{\omega}{c}(n_0 - n_x)\mathrm{d}s$$

to give

$$\frac{\mathrm{d}\Omega}{\mathrm{d}s} = \tfrac{1}{2}\frac{\omega}{c}XY = \frac{NBe^2}{8\pi^2 m_e^2 c\epsilon_0 f^2}.$$

Provided the total Faraday rotation angle, Ω, is experimentally found then the total electron content along the path, $\int N\,\mathrm{d}s$ can be calculated, since all the terms in this equation, except for B, N and Ω are known constants. In the ionosphere B does not vary too much so that it can also be treated as a constant.

4.6. *Communications*

If we want to send a radio wave from point A to point B then some of the ways we can do it are illustrated in fig. 4.9. If A and B are separated by a large distance then the curvature of the Earth becomes important and the direct signal cannot reach B which is below the horizon. The two (or more) radio signals that arrive at B are unlikely to have the same phase so that they interfere with each other. The ionosphere is constantly changing so that the phase difference between the two waves is also constantly changing. This produces the alternate periods of loudness and silence, known as fading, that is so familiar to all short wave radio listeners. Local radio transmissions within a city produce good reception because the direct wave is received, but the frequency is low enough (~ 800 kHz) to absorb the reflected wave so that interference and its consequent fading will not occur. Frequency modulated, FM, transmission is conducted at such a high frequency that there is no reflected wave at all; it passes right through the ionosphere. The best short wave transmission occurs when the one-hop reflected wave is the only one to arrive. This can be achieved either by making sure that the two-hop signal is heavily absorbed or by choosing the frequencies so that the one-hop signal is reflected and the two-hop signal is not reflected but passes right through the ionosphere.

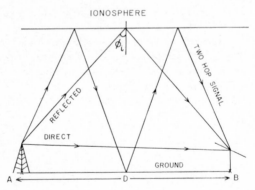

Fig. 4.9. Some ways of sending a radio signal from A to B.

The reason we can do this is that the critical frequency of radio wave reflection does not only depend on the critical plasma frequency, it also depends on the angle at which the radio wave strikes the ionosphere. The situation is analogous to the total internal reflection of light. Imagine a radio wave—as in fig. 4.9—striking the ionosphere at an angle ϕ_i to the normal. In practice the wave will not be immediately reflected but will penetrate a certain distance into the

78

ionosphere before it is reflected. If we think of the angle ϕ as representing the angle which the wave makes with the normal, then ϕ will vary from ϕ_i to $90°$ ($\pi/2$ radians) and then back to ϕ_i. The angles will obey Snell's law $n \sin \phi = $ constant. At the bottom of the ionosphere the refractive index is that of free space, $n = 1$, and the angle is ϕ_i so that

$$n \sin \phi = \sin \phi_i$$

At the top of the wave's trajectory, when it is reflected $\phi = 90°$, and we shall use n_R to denote the refractive index when the wave is reflected.

$$n_R = \sin \phi_i$$

If we follow only the ordinary wave in a reflection from the F region then we would be justified in neglecting both collisions and the magnetic field. Then we can write an expression for n_R based on equation 4.1

$$n_R{}^2 = 1 - \frac{(f_0)^2}{f^2} = \sin^2 \phi_i$$

so that the frequency at which the wave is reflected is

$$f = \frac{f_0}{\sqrt{(1 - \sin^2 \phi_i)}} = \frac{f_0}{\cos \phi_i} = f_0 \sec \phi_i$$

where f_0 is the ordinary wave critical frequency of the layer we are dealing with.

For example, on the ionogram of fig. 4.6 $f_0 F2$ was 7·4 MHz. Waves below this frequency are reflected, waves above this frequency pass right through the ionosphere, provided that the radio wave strikes the ionosphere at right angles ($\phi_i = 0°$). For long distance transmission, if ϕ_i is 45° then sec $\phi_i = \sqrt{2}$. In this case waves up to 10 MHz will be reflected. The greater the angle, the higher the frequency that can be reflected. The limit is reached when the angle is so great that the wave is going through a large amount of the D region. Then absorption will dissipate the wave.

The maximum usable frequency

When sending radio transmissions between two points it is wise to calculate the maximum usable frequency (MUF) and to choose the actual operating frequency just below this. To calculate the MUF, one needs to know the distance to the transmitting station and the state of the ionosphere. Let us imagine that I wanted to send a radio message at noon on April 14, 1965 from Accra, the capital of Ghana, to the Saharan town of Timbuktu in the republic of Mali. The distance between Accra and Timbuktu is 2000 km.

79

We know the state of the ionosphere. This is represented by an ionogram, and the ionogram for that date and time is reproduced in fig. 4.6. We are going to need to use Breit and Tuve's theorem:

The time for a radio wave to travel from a transmitter (A) to a receiver (B) by means of an ionospheric reflection is the same as if the radio wave were reflected by a mirror situated at the virtual height, h'.

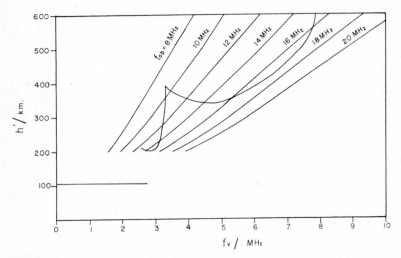

Fig. 4.10. Family of fixed frequency transmission curves for a fixed distance of 2000 km superimposed on the ionogram of fig. 4.6. A flat earth and flat ionosphere are assumed.

The height at which the reflections in fig. 4.9 occur will increase as the wave frequency increases. The relationship between oblique and equivalent-vertical frequencies in the case of a mirror at a height h', for transmission over a distance D, is given by

$$f_{ob} = f_v \sec \phi_i = f_v \sqrt{\left[1 + \left(\frac{D}{2h'} \right)^2 \right]} \qquad (4.5)$$

But f_v and h' are not independent. An ionogram gives one in terms of the other.

To find the MUF we graph curves of constant f_{ob} onto an ionogram. These curves are known as transmission curves and they are drawn in fig. 4.10 when $D = 2000$ km. When D and f_{ob} are held constant, equation 4.5 links f_v and h' and gives the transmission curves. Since they do not depend on the state of the ionosphere they can be put onto transparent paper and put over an actual ionogram.

80

We are interested in the intersection of the transmission curves and the ionogram. The ordinary trace of the ionogram has been redrawn in fig. 4.10 onto a linear scale. Certain transmission curves intersect with the ionogram trace. Each point of intersection represents a reflected wave that will reach Timbuktu, and the virtual height of reflection for the wave can be read off the graph. A frequency of 16 MHz, for example, can reach Timbuktu along two different paths through the F2 region; one low angle transmission (i.e. high ϕ_i) corresponding to mirror reflection at 340 km altitude and a high angle transmission being reflected, at about 550 km altitude. A 12 MHz signal would reach Timbuktu by means of a low-angle transmission via the F1 layer ($h' = 280$ km) or a high-angle transmission via the F2 layer ($h' = 350$ km). E region transmissions can also be produced but they will suffer from absorption so we will disregard them. The actual ray paths for some of these points are shown in fig. 4.11.

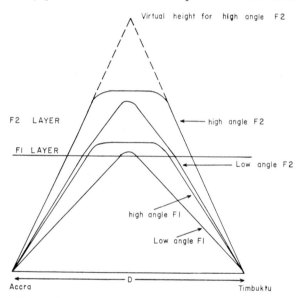

Fig. 4.11. Ray paths corresponding to intersections of transmission curves and ionograms.

The MUF can be found by looking for the frequency at which the ionogram is tangential to a transmission curve. At this point only one ray path is possible, focusing takes place and the received signal will be enhanced. In our example the maximum usable frequency is 17 MHz. Since this is for a 2000 km transmission via the F2 layer, it is written

$$\text{MUF (2000) F2} = 17 \text{ MHz}$$

81

Provided that one knows the F2 region plasma frequency—which we could write as MUF (ZERO) F2—and MUF (D) F2 then one can calculate the MUF for any distance between zero and D km. To help broadcasters, many governments publish ionospheric predictions three months in advance giving world maps of the predicted MUF (ZERO) F2 and MUF (4000) F2 for every two hours. Commercial broadcasters choose their operating frequencies by taking 0·85 of the monthly average MUF for the distance they wish to transmit to. This means that every month the frequency that a short wave radio station uses will change. All the major short wave broadcasters (BBC World Service, Voice of America, Radio Moscow, Deutsche Welle, etc.) issue monthly bulletins telling their listeners which frequencies they will be operating the next month.

Skip zone

Let us assume that we have chosen some operating frequency and our transmitter is working at this fixed frequency. In fig. 4.12 we see what happens to the ray path as the angle of elevation slowly increases. For low angles the propagation path 1 is long. As the elevation increases, the ground range (path 2) decreases until a minimum is reached at the point C, after which the range increases rapidly as shown by paths 4 and 5. Eventually, penetration of the ionosphere occurs as shown by path 6.

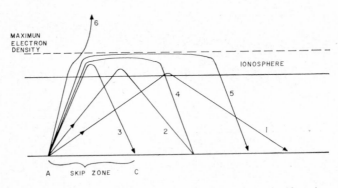

Fig. 4.12. Ray paths for fixed frequency transmission as the elevation varies.

It is impossible to send a radio wave by means of ionospheric reflections to any point closer to the transmitter than point C. This area which cannot be reached is called the skip zone. We can see that ray 3 combines both the high-angle and low-angle transmissions for propagation from A to C so that the frequency used must be the

82

maximum usable frequency for propagation from A to C. Thus on April 14, 1965 the skip zone for a 17 MHz wave from Accra corresponded to 2000 km.

Satellites

The first artificial satellite, Sputnik, sent up by the U.S.S.R. in 1957 did no more than radio back to the Earth a succession of blips. The Chinese did somewhat better with their first satellite in 1970. It cheerfully sang their national anthem ' The East is Red ' and extolled the virtues of Chairman Mao Tse Tung. Since Sputnik, the satellites in orbit have become more sophisticated and more specialized. The first satellite to take topside ionograms was the Canadian satellite Alouette launched in 1962. This was followed by the American Explorer 17, devoted solely to taking aeronomy measurements. Communications received a great boost the following year when Syncom 3 was the first satellite to be put into a geostationary orbit,

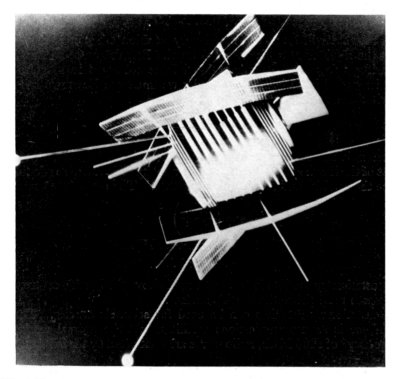

Fig. 4.13. America's Explorer 38 satellite is being used for scientific research. It is recording the low frequency radio waves found in the magnetosphere. (Photo by USIS.)

i.e. it remained fixed over one location on the Earth. Nowadays, satellites perform all manner of exotic functions ranging from spying on enemy missile sites to monitoring the polar bear population of the Arctic. Miniature radio transmitters are attached to some of the bears and their movements followed via satellite. The Earth Resources Technology Satellites photograph the Earth's flora and keep a check on the Earth's temperature by taking infrared photographs. To illustrate the sheer volume of floating hardware in the sky, the Appendix lists the satellites launched in two months of 1972. Twenty-six of them!

We can see that satellites are playing a vital role in both our scientific understanding of the upper atmosphere and in improving our methods of communication. Aeronomical information from orbiting satellites comes from observing the changes in their rate of revolution—providing a measure of the atmospheric density; from their ability to take topside ionograms which give information on the upper ionosphere, and from their ability to make direct measurements on the temperature, magnetic field, particle composition, etc., of the region of space in which they are orbiting.

A satellite will be in a geostationary position when it is in orbit over the Equator at a distance r from the Earth's centre so that its centrifugal force and its gravitational force are equal in magnitude and its period is 24 hours. To find r we must use Newton's law of gravitation so that

$$m\Omega_E{}^2 r = \frac{GM_E m}{r^2}$$

where m is the satellite's mass, G the gravitational constant, M_E the mass of the Earth and Ω_E is the angular velocity of the Earth's rotation, since the satellite and Earth rotate together. Thus

$$r = \left(\frac{GM_E}{\Omega_E{}^2}\right)^{1/3}$$
$$= \sqrt[3]{(75\cdot4 \times 10^{21})} \text{ m}$$
$$= 4\cdot22 \times 10^7 \text{ m.}$$

A geostationary satellite is 6·6 Earth radii above the Earth's centre, or 5·6 Earth radii above the Earth's surface.

Geostationary satellites can be used for scientific studies. Their main use is as communications satellites. At the normal working frequency* of 5000 MHz, radio waves are unaffected by the ionosphere

* For example, the Intelsat IV satellite receives in the 5925–6425 MHz band from the ground stations, amplifies the signals by a factor of 10^9 and retransmits them down in the 3700–4200 MHz band. This series of satellites handles 5000 telephone circuits and several television channels.

and can be sent from one part of the world to another via the satellite which acts as a relay station. The advent of geostationary satellites is revolutionizing communications in the developing countries. For the continent of Africa, or for the subcontinent of India, it is a far more economical proposition to pay for a satellite and to build satellite receiving stations than to build extensive microwave transmission facilities.

For this reason both Brazil and India have thriving space programmes. Current plans are to put a geostationary satellite over India by 1976. Forty major satellite receiving centres have already been built and these centres will relay the television and radio broadcasts that they pick up to over two hundred villages, which would otherwise not be able to have any television reception. You can see that we have a paradoxical situation. It is cheaper in this case for the developing countries to use highly sophisticated technology and by-pass all the intermediate steps. This leads to the anomalous position where a country with a large illiterate population and with great medical and agricultural problems, such as India, nevertheless has a thriving space programme. By providing better communications it will be easier to educate the peasants in public health and modern agriculture and help eliminate the worst aspects of inequality.

4.7. *Low and very low frequency transmissions*

Much of this chapter has been devoted to discussing high frequency (h.f.) propagation because of its importance in amateur and commercial short wave broadcasting. The chief advantage of high frequencies is the relative simplicity of the transmitting and receiving equipment and the fact that it can be used for long distance communication. Unfortunately, h.f. propagation is unreliable during ionospheric disturbances and it can suffer from rapid and deep fading of the signal, as every short wave listener knows. These defects in h.f. propagation can be largely overcome by the use of low and very low frequencies (l.f. and v.l.f.).

The chief disadvantage of l.f. and v.l.f. transmission are the large, and hence expensive, transmitters that are needed to overcome the high radio noise on v.l.f. The requisite aerials are so vast that the world's v.l.f. stations are some of the largest man-made structures. Current interest in v.l.f. is mainly military, because these frequencies penetrate through 10 metres of water and hence allow communications with submarines, and also because they are relatively unaffected by nuclear bursts in the atmosphere—which tend to mess up h.f. communications.

Very low frequency propagation operates by successive reflections from the D region and the ground. Both of these act as good mirrors for v.l.f. waves so that the reflected waves are very stable both in phase and in amplitude. Propagation of v.l.f. is so regular that each transmitter has its ' pole' on the opposite side of the globe where the waves come together again in phase. This extreme regularity of signal propagation, combined with the system's military advantages, led the Americans to build a v.l.f. navigation system called Omega. This uses eight transmitters situated around the globe. The signal from any three can be used to determine one's position to within five kilometres.

Generally speaking, in times of nuclear attack any v.l.f. station is likely to be high on the enemy's target list. Originally the United States had intended to build an Omega station in the South Island of New Zealand, but they had to abandon this plan when strong local protest forced the New Zealand Government to withhold permission.

The Omega system is meant to replace the ageing l.f. navigation systems such as Decca, Loran and Consol. Since l.f. propagation is characterized by more absorption during reflections and less radio noise in comparison to v.l.f. it was used for these intermediate range navigation systems. As the l.f. receiving equipment is much cheaper than v.l.f. receiving equipment it is likely to be quite a while before the Omega system completely replaces the existing l.f. networks.

Further reading:

Davies, K., 1969.   *Ionospheric Radio Waves, Blaisdell.*   (Waltham, Massachusetts: Xerox College Publishing.)

Davies, K., 1966.   *Ionospheric Radio Propagation.*   (New York: Dover.)

Kelso, John M., 1964.   *Radio Ray Propagation in the Ionosphere.*   (New York: McGraw-Hill.)

These books are quite advanced mathematically, and I have tried to arrange them in order of increasing difficulty. The two classical reference works on radio waves in the ionosphere are:

Budden, K. G., 1961.   *Radio Waves in the Ionosphere.*   (Cambridge University Press.)

Ratcliffe, J. A., 1962.   *Magneto-Ionic Theory.*   (Cambridge University Press.)

A short survey of radio frequency applications is given by:

Laurie, P., 1974.   No room in the radio spectrum, *New Scientist*, **62,** 533–536.

5.1. *Ionospheric temperature*

WE have seen that the ionosphere is caused by the radiation from the Sun. This can ionize the constituent gases, depending upon two factors: the wavelength of the radiation and the properties of the absorbing gas. The radiation must be able to penetrate the atmosphere above the ionized layer and then be absorbed in that layer. Furthermore, the wavelength must be shorter than a critical value (which varies from one gas to another), for without this condition, electrons will not be ejected from the atoms.

The temperature of any gas—be it oxygen, nitrogen, an electron gas or an ion gas—is determined by the distribution of random particle velocities. When an atom absorbs a photon and emits an electron, these free electrons have much higher velocities than either the ions or the neutrals. If we apply the law of conservation of linear momentum we will see that when the electron is ejected the remaining ion must recoil. This means that the ion's velocity will be greater than the un-ionized particle's velocity but not as great as the electron's velocity since the lighter electron has a greater velocity when both momenta are equal.

Particle temperatures in the atmosphere will depend on particle velocities, and we can see that the electron, ion and neutral temperatures are not necessarily equal because the velocity distributions of the three species are not the same. Once the electron has been ejected from a neutral un-ionized particle, the final temperature will depend on the collision frequencies (Table 1.2). In the F region during the daytime, electron–ion collisions are numerous but electron–neutral collisions are rare. Hence overall, electrons will transfer much of their kinetic energy to ions, but very little to neutrals. For the daytime F region we can write

$$T_e > T_i > T_n$$

where subscripts e, i and n represent electron, ion and neutral gas temperatures respectively. This inequality is not true in the D and E regions where all three temperatures are equal. In the lower ionosphere, collisions between electrons and neutrals and between ions and neutrals are so frequent that electrons, ions and neutral very quickly share their velocities.

At night there is no solar radiation so that there are no ejected electrons. The ionosphere diminishes in concentration and collisions equalize the electron, ion and neutral temperatures in all the ionospheric regions.

These results on the ionospheric temperatures were obtained by a technique, pioneered in 1958, called incoherent-scatter radar. This measures the scattering of radar signals by individual electrons and only became possible after the development of extremely high-powered radar. The basis of the incoherent-scatter radar is that if a radio wave of frequency f_0 strikes an electron, then the electron will re-radiate the wave at a Doppler-shifted frequency

$$f = \frac{f_0}{1 \pm (V/c)}$$

that depends on the velocity (V) of the electron, which in turn depends on the electron temperature. Since there will be a distribution of electron velocities, there will be a distribution of incoherent scattered frequencies.

At first, the theorists had predicted that the distribution of frequencies would have a peak at the transmitting frequency f_0. When the experimental results were analysed a completely different result appeared (fig. 5.1). The observed spread of frequencies has two humps which depend on the ratio of the electron temperature (T_e) to the ion temperature (T_i). The electron temperature controls the width of the resulting two-humped spectrum, the ratio T_e/T_i controls the height of the wings, and the actual power returned can be used to measure the electron density, N. An incoherent-scatter radar can measure these parameters from 100 km up to 1000 km or more.

Routine measurements made with incoherent scatter radars have produced some unexpected results. The inequality of the F region electron, ion and neutral temperatures was one of these. Another one was the discovery that the F region temperatures would sometimes show a sudden increase an hour or so before dawn. The cause of this was subsequently shown to be the arrival of fast electrons following the magnetic field lines from the opposite hemisphere. When solar radiation starts to strike the upper F region in Alaska, a large number of energetic electrons is suddenly produced. The electrons that move downwards strike the neutral atmosphere and increase T_n. The electrons that move upwards have no significant atmosphere to collide with so they travel along, guided by the magnetic field lines, until they strike the dark F region in New Zealand—the geomagnetic conjugate*

---

* Two points at opposite ends of a magnetic field line are called geomagnetic conjugates. This is fully dealt with in Section 6.3.

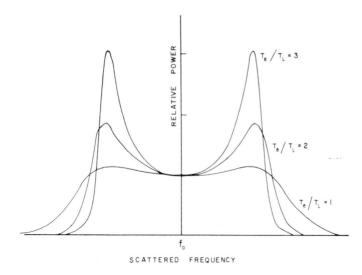

Fig. 5.1. The actual results of incoherent scatter radar experiments. f_0 is frequency at which the original signal is transmitted.

to Alaska. This increases the F region temperature in New Zealand a few hours before daybreak would be expected to.

5.2. *The F region* (above 150 km)

Much of the dynamics of the ionosphere can be explained by assuming that there is no movement of ionization. In this case, the equation of continuity

$$\frac{dN}{dt} = q - L$$

relates the changes in electron concentration to the ionization production rate (q) and the loss rate (L). The loss rate is determined by the chemistry of the ionosphere and, in the F region, we have seen that

$$L = \beta N$$

where β is the attachment-like coefficient (see p. 35). The photochemistry of the ionosphere was dealt with in Chapter 2, but fig. 5.2 summarizes the major reactions in greater detail. The separation of the ionosphere into E and F regions occurs because of the change in chemistry at the two heights.

We have also seen that two separate F layers show up on daytime ionograms (fig. 4.6)—the F1 layer in summer at about 200 km and

89

the much more dense F2 layer at about 300 km. The existence of these two layers cannot be explained as a consequence of different ionization rates or losses, but the two layers can be explained when the movement of ionization is included.

The F1 layer, when it is observed on ionograms, approximates the behaviour of a Chapman α layer, indicating that the F1 layer lies at the transition between the $L = \alpha N^2$ and $L = \beta N$ loss formulae. The

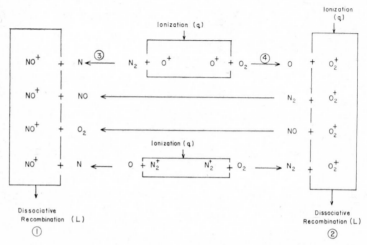

Fig. 5.2.   The ion-chemistry of the E and F regions.

F1 layer is a curious hybrid in which atomic ions are being produced but the principal loss mechanism is dissociative recombination with a molecular ion.

There is no known solar radiation that is capable of causing a peak of q production at 300 km. In fact, the peak of production occurs at the F1 layer. Actually the F2 layer is a peak of N, not of q, and it was once thought that the rapid decrease of β with height accounted for the F2 layer. After many theoretical attempts to derive an F2 layer on this basis, it became apparent that diffusion was controlling the F2 layer whose peak occurs at the height where diffusion and loss are of equal importance.

Diffusion
As long as a gas is homogeneous no diffusion will occur. However, if there is a greater quantity of the gas at one location, then the pressure there will be greater and the gas will diffuse away from the region of high concentration in an attempt to equalize the pressures.

90

The concepts of diffusion and viscosity are both molecular transport processes. They are intimately related. Viscosity occurs because molecules transfer their momentum to other molecules with less momentum.

In an un-ionized gas the coefficient of diffusion, D, is related to the coefficient of viscosity (μ) by

$$D = \eta/\rho = \mu$$

so that the coefficient of kinematic viscosity μ is an exact measure of diffusion.*

The diffusion of an ionized gas is not so straightforward, because the effects of electric and magnetic fields have to be taken into account. In the case of the ionosphere we are interested primarily in vertical diffusion, which process controls the height distribution of electron density. At the magnetic equator, vertical diffusion of ions and electrons cannot take place. The magnetic field is horizontal and the particles are held in place by the magnetic field so that vertical movement cannot occur unless it is caused by the presence of electric fields (which we would call drift, not diffusion). Horizontal diffusion along the magnetic field line is, however, possible.

At the magnetic poles, the magnetic field is vertical and so vertical diffusion becomes possible. Since the gas pressure is the force component per unit area, the vertical derivative of the pressure is going to be the diffusive force per unit volume. To account for diffusion we can write the vertical equation of motion for ions as

$$\frac{\mathrm{d}}{\mathrm{d}z}(NkT_i) = -Nm_i g + NeE - Nm_i \nu_{in}(V_z - U_z)$$

and for electrons as

$$\frac{\mathrm{d}}{\mathrm{d}z}(NkT_e) = -Nm_e g - NeE - Nm_e \nu_{en}(V_z - U_z)$$

vertical diffusive force	gravity	electric force	collisions with neutrals

where the NkT term is the plasma pressure, the product Nm is the plasma density, and k is the Boltzmann constant.

From simple kinetic theory we know that when a particle hits another one and recoils, the force exerted on it is equal to the change

---

* At this level of treatment, D and μ are identical. At a more advanced evel, D is a tensor but μ is a scalar.

of momentum of the particle divided by the duration of collision—that is in effect multiplied by the number of collisions in unit time. Thus, in the case of electron–neutral collisions, the force per unit volume due to the collisions is the product of the number of electrons per unit volume, N, their mass, m_e, the collision frequency ν_{en} and the relative velocity of the electrons with respect to the neutrals: $\mathbf{V} - \mathbf{U}$. Since this force is due to a recoil it acts in the direction opposite to the relative velocity and hence is preceded by a minus sign. As can be seen, a similar term describes the ion–neutral collisional force.

These equations have been simplified by assuming that the electrons and ions drift together so that they both have the same vertical drift V_z. We can further simplify the equations by assuming the neutral atmosphere is stationary so that $U_z = 0$ and by assuming that collisions with neutral particles are more important for the ions so $m_i \nu_{in} \gg m_e \nu_{en}$. On adding the equations, the terms in E vanish and because of Newton's third law, so do the ion–electron collision terms which were omitted from the equations because they are negligible anyway. Rearranging to solve for the drift velocity of the plasma

$$V_z = -\frac{1}{m_i \nu_{in}} \left\{ \frac{1}{N} \frac{d}{dz} [Nk(T_i + T_e)] + m_i g \right\}$$

where the minus sign indicates that the drift is in the opposite direction to the electron density gradient causing it. The gravitational force on the electrons can be ignored in comparison to the gravitational force on the ions.

This equation can be written in a more convenient form if we define the 'plasma temperature', T_p, by

$$T_p = \tfrac{1}{2}(T_i + T_e)$$

and the 'plasma scale height' H_p by

$$H_p = \frac{2kT_p}{m_i g},$$

which is equivalent to regarding the plasma as a gas in which the mean particle mass is $\tfrac{1}{2}m_i$, on account of the negligible mass of the electrons. After some rearrangement, we can write

$$V_z = -D \left[\frac{1}{N} \frac{dN}{dz} + \frac{1}{T_p} \frac{dT_p}{dz} + \frac{1}{H_p} \right] \tag{5.1}$$

where we introduce the 'plasma diffusion coefficient' D and define it as

$$D = \frac{2kT_p}{m_i \nu_{in}} \left.\right\} \text{plasma diffusion}$$

This is very similar to the coefficient of kinematic viscosity that can be worked out by using kinetic theory, for which

$$\mu = \frac{8}{3\pi} \frac{kT_n}{m\nu_{nn}} \left.\right\} \text{neutral gas diffusion}$$

where ν_{nn} is the classical collision frequency between uncharged molecules of the same gas.

Diffusion will also affect the continuity equation. The transport of charged particles in the vertical direction is given by the derivative of the flux of particles, where the flux is the number crossing unit area in unit time, so that the continuity equation becomes

$$\frac{dN}{dt} = q - L - \frac{d(NV_z)}{dz} \tag{5.2}$$

In the F region $L = \beta N$, and the diffusion coefficient increases exponentially with height because ν_{in} decreases exponentially with height. In this case, some quite complicated mathematics reveals that

(a) The F2 peak (i.e. when $\frac{dN}{dz} = 0$) occurs when diffusion and loss are of comparable importance, i.e. where $\beta \sim D/H^2$, where H is the neutral scale height.

(b) At the F2 peak the electron concentration is given by $N \sim q/\beta$, just as it would be in the absence of diffusion.

(c) Well above the peak, the electron distribution is exponential.

F region anomalies

All the ionospheric layers show gross departures from the behaviour that one would expect in relation to the Sun. Though the D, E and F layers do often show the regular changes that one associates with the sunspot cycle and with the variation in the inclination of the Sun, χ, there are certain phenomena which cannot be adequately described by the single continuity equation (5.2) when the vertical drift is given by a form of equation (5.1) that allows for non-vertical magnetic fields. Departures from the structure predicted by this approach were originally called anomalies, mainly to conceal ignorance of the true

93

state of affairs. Some of these anomalies have since been successfully explained; some have not.

Anomalies might be expected at high latitudes where solar irradiation is weak, but they also occur at temperate and low latitudes. Very marked anomalies occur during 'ionospheric storms' which accompany perturbations of the Earth's magnetic field that result from disturbances on the Sun. Even when there is no magnetic disturbance the ionosphere displays several anomalies which will be discussed in various parts of this chapter.

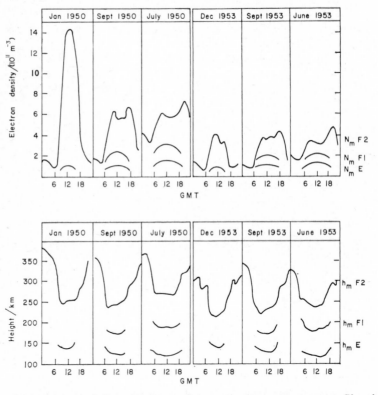

Fig. 5.3. Average daily variations of ionospheric parameters at Slough, England during six representative months. 1950 was a year of high solar activity, 1953 one of low solar activity. *Above:* peak electron densities of the F2, F1 and E layers. *Below:* height of the peaks of these layers. Note that the F1 layer is not seen in winter.

The major temperate latitude F region anomalies are shown in fig. 5.3. This figure shows the average peak electron densities and heights of the F2, F1 and E layers at Slough, England during three

94

months of a year of high sunspot number (1950) and a year of low sunspot number (1953). The anomalies in this figure are:

(i) The F2 seasonal anomaly.

During January, 1950—a winter month when χ would be very high—the peak F2 electron density was much higher than it was during the summer or autumn. To further complicate matters, in the southern hemisphere the anomaly takes a semi-annual form, with maximum f_0 F2 occurring in spring and autumn.

A complete explanation of the seasonal anomaly has not yet been offered. The best suggestion so far claims that there may be a seasonal change in the neutral atmospheric composition decreasing the proportion of the molecular gas and reducing the loss coefficient β. The main problem with this explanation is that it fails to explain why the anomaly does not also occur at night.

(ii) The diurnal variation in the F2 peak.

Whereas January, 1950 has an electron density that reaches a maximum value at noon, all of the other figures have a ' noon bite-out ' producing two maxima; one in the morning and one in the afternoon. There are two alternate explanations for this, one based on the variations in T_e produced at the magnetically conjugate point and the other attributing the diurnal variation to the thermospheric winds.

(iii) The disappearing F1 layer.

When the F1 layer is visible, it varies quite regularly with χ. During winter and during periods of very high solar activity it is not visible. The reason for this seems to be closely related to the seasonal anomaly in the F2 layer. When the F2 layer has an exceedingly high peak of electron density then the whole F2 region has an enhanced electron density and the F1 ledge is swamped by the increased ionization.

5.3. *The E region* (90 km–150 km)

The normal E region is produced by the Sun's X-rays and ultraviolet radiation, and during the daytime there is a balance between the production of charged particles and the dissociative recombinations that act as a sink for the charged particles. The daytime E region behaves almost exactly like a Chapman α layer so that most of its normal features are well understood.

If we try to solve the continuity equation for the night-time E region then we would be led to predict that the whole E region should recombine and disappear by midnight. This does not happen. The E region persists throughout the whole night with an electron density of 10^9 m^{-3}, which is about two orders of magnitude lower than the daytime value but is still far from negligible. (An electron density below 10^8 m^{-3} is considered as being negligible.) The ionization above the E region peak decays faster than the ionization at the peak itself so that a characteristic night-time E region valley occurs, with a local minimum of ionization at approximately 135 km.

The most probable explanation for the tenacity of the night-time E region peak is that long-lived metallic ions, Fe^+, Mg^+, Na^+, etc., dominate the night-time recombination processes once most shorter lived NO^+ and O^+ ions have disappeared. It is most likely that meteors deposit the long-lived metallic ions into the 90 to 110 km height range, but experiments designed to check this have not been successful. As yet, no good correlation between meteor showers and the magnitude of the peak has been found.

Sporadic E

The most important type of ionospheric anomaly at E region heights is sporadic E, normally abbreviated to E_s. This is a very thin layer of very dense ionization (fig. 5.4) occurring at random, which can play havoc with radio communications.

On December 30, 1971 an Australian newspaper, the *Sydney Morning Herald*, carried this story:

Hobart calls for Sydney taxis

During unusual ionospheric conditions yesterday, Sydney taxi-drivers found themselves being requested by Hobart ' callers ' to proceed to various Hobart suburbs.

At the same time, Hobart drivers were experiencing the same confusion as they were instructed to pick up fares at Sydney Airport.

Popular theories among the drivers are that the signals are transmitted by sunspots, or caused by special atmospheric conditions.

The Editor of *Electronics Australia*, Mr. J. Rowe, said yesterday the taxi-drivers were not far from the truth in their theories.

The phenomena were due to unusual activity in the ' E ' layer of the Earth's ionosphere. Mr. Rowe said that although not too much was known about this activity, known as ' Sporadic E ', it had been wondered at for years.

To understand this freak radio transmission we must think in terms of the transmission curves and maximum usable frequencies that were introduced in Chapter 4. A really intense daytime sporadic E layer can have a critical frequency, $f_x E_s$, which is greater than the maximum F2 region critical frequency, $f_x F2$. But the sporadic E layer is usually at a height of about 100 to 120 km, and like the normal E region it produces an echo that is a straight line—none of the cusps and kinks that we see on the F1 and F2 traces.

Imagine a straight line drawn on fig. 4.10 at a height of 120 km extending from 0 Hz to 8 Hz. It is not difficult to see that this is going to increase the maximum usable frequency, MUF (2000) E_s, tremendously. We can see from fig. 2.2 that 1965 was a year of low solar activity. During a year of high solar activity like 1971 there are many more electrons in the ionosphere, f_0F2 increases, MUF (2000) F2 increases, f_xE_s increases and so does MUF (2000) E_s. For intense sporadic E at high solar activity the maximum usable frequency

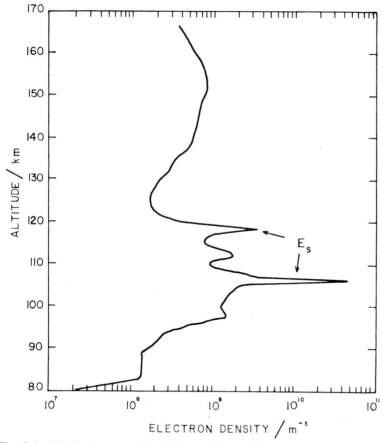

Fig. 5.4. Night-time sporadic E layers observed by a rocket. An intense sporadic E layer can be fifty times denser than the rest of the E region. Only the lower layer would show up on an ionosonde.

for a 2000 km transmission can exceed 100 MHz. Radio taxis use frequencies in this range so that at high solar activity when sporadic E occurs, microwave and television reception can be disrupted by signals from very far away.

When does sporadic E occur? We cannot fully answer this question for the onset of temperate latitude sporadic E is determined by neutral winds in the E region. Equatorial E_s and polar E_s have different causes that we will deal with later.

Temperate E_s occurs when there is a shear in the horizontal wind. If there is an eastward wind at one height and a westward wind at another height then the charged particles will converge into a thin layer. The way this happens is as follows: The neutral particles of the wind collide with the charged particles and set them moving. However, the charged particles start circling around the almost horizontal magnetic field line. In the E region, large numbers of neutral–charged particle collisions take place so charged particles are not even able to complete one half a revolution before they are pushed on by the neutral wind. The overall motion is as shown in fig. 5.5. One set of particles moves downwards at a slant and another set moves upwards at a slant. This is the wind shear mechanism of sporadic E formation. If we could predict when the wind shears occur, then we could predict when sporadic E is going to occur.

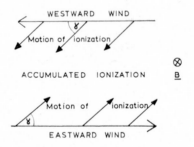

Fig. 5.5. The wind shear mechanism of sporadic E formation at temperate latitudes.

5.4. *The D region* (60 km–90 km)

The D region is the least understood of the ionospheric regions. It is formed by the ionization initiated by solar X-rays, galactic cosmic rays (which are X-radiations from some unknown source in outer space), and most importantly by the absorption of the 121·6 nm Lyman-α radiation from the Sun by nitric oxide, NO. Once formed, however, it has a highly complex chemistry, made even more complex by the presence of negative ions and water cluster ions. There is no simple expression for the D region loss rate.

Even the structure of the D region is in dispute. Ground-based experiments on the D region give the structure shown in fig. 1.6; there is a kink in the electron density profile at 75 km which is sometimes called the C layer. Rockets shot through the D region do not find any kink at 75 km, and we do not know which technique is correct. Luckily both techniques agree that at night the D region disappears. Since the D region is responsible for most of the absorption of radio waves, radio reception improves dramatically at night.

The Luxembourg effect

The Luxembourg effect was discovered in the 1930's when radio listeners in Holland found that their reception from Radio Paris, Budapest and Milan was getting mixed up with the very powerful broadcasts from Radio Luxembourg. The surprising thing about this was that the frequencies of the two stations that were interacting were completely different.

The cause of the Luxembourg effect lies in the D region. When a very powerful radio wave, like that of Radio Luxembourg, passes through the D region it heats the free electrons because it increases their velocities. In fact the electron temperature faithfully follows the amplitude of the powerful wave. When it is strong, T_e is high, when it is weak T_e returns to its normal D region value.

The electron–neutral collision frequency,* ν, depends on the temperature of both species. When T_e increases, so does ν. So that when a powerful radio wave goes through the D region, the collision frequency ν will be proportional to the amplitude of the powerful wave.

If a weaker wave goes through the ionosphere at the same time as the powerful wave, then the absorption of the weaker wave will depend on the value of ν, the collision frequency in the D region. Thus the weaker wave will have its amplitude modulated by the variations in ν, which happen to be the same as the variations in amplitude of the powerful wave. So people on the ground listening to the weaker station will find themselves listening to a jumbled intermixing of the two stations.

The Luxembourg effect provides us with a method of studying the D region. Since the absorption coefficient in the D region depends on both the electron density, N, and the collision frequency, ν, accurate measurements of the wave interaction can be used to find both N and ν.

* As this is the most commonly used collision frequency it is normally written without a subscript.

Sudden ionospheric disturbances

Near the sunspot maximum of 1937 a particularly interesting anomalous feature of radio wave absorption was noticed for the first time. It took the form of a very sudden increase of absorption followed by a slower return to normal, the whole change usually lasting an hour and occurring only in daytime. It was given the name sudden ionospheric disturbance, usually abbreviated to SID.

It soon became apparent that SIDs were caused by a sudden increase in the number of solar flares. This abrupt increase in solar activity increased the amount of very energetic X-radiation reaching the ionosphere, and this highly penetrating radiation increased the D region ionization and hence the radio wave absorption. A burst of radiation of this kind would ionize only on the daylight side of the ionosphere and it was only there that SIDs were observed.

During a SID the absorption of medium and high frequency radio waves is often great enough to result in the complete removal of a signal reflected from the E or F layers. It is then said that there is a short wave fade-out (SWF).

5.5. *The equatorial ionosphere*

Once routine monitoring of the ionosphere had become widespread, it soon became apparent that certain aspects of the behaviour of the equatorial ionosphere differed greatly from the behaviour of the ionosphere elsewhere. These differences were not determined by the geographical equator, but were related to the dip equator where the magnetic field is always completely horizontal. Much of the behaviour in the equatorial ionosphere arises because the charged particles are held in place by the magnetic field line so that vertical diffusion cannot occur.

The dip, or magnetic, equator coincides with the geographic equator at only two points—in the mid-Pacific and mid-Atlantic oceans. From Central Africa to India the dip equator closely follows the $10°$ N parallel but in South America it reaches as far south as $15°$ S.

Certain features of the equatorial ionosphere, such as the E region electron density profile, do not differ greatly from the mid-latitude ionosphere, so that in this section I shall only present some of its unique features.

The equatorial electrojet

Magnetic field measurements near the dip equator show an abnormally large amplitude for the daily variation of the horizontal component of the Earth's magnetic field. This enhancement is believed to be caused by an electric current of about 300 km in width flowing in the dynamo region above the dip equator. This current is called the equatorial electrojet.

100

The basic reason for the existence of the electrojet is that the east–west conductivity (the Cowling conductivity) has a very large value near the dip equator. Since the current in the dynamo region is proportional to the product of the conductivity and the electric field there, a small electric field can produce an appreciable current. This in turn means that the drift velocities of the charged particles responsible for the current will be large and since these charged particles collide with neutral particles, there will be an appreciable wind accompanying the electrojet (fig. 3.5). The Cowling conductivity drops appreciably at night and the equatorial electrojet almost disappears.

Electrons and ions in the electrojet move in opposite directions. If they have a very large relative velocity then the interface between them becomes unstable and the plasma becomes turbulent. This shows up on equatorial ionosondes as equatorial sporadic E. It is a direct consequence of the existence of the electrojet. When the electrojet disappears at night, so does equatorial sporadic E.

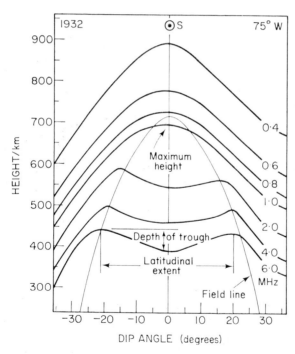

Fig. 5.6. A model of the equatorial anomaly based on topside ionograms from satellites. The graph shows the height at which a fixed frequency is reflected.

101

The equatorial anomaly

When the F2 region critical frequency is plotted against dip angle, or against magnetic latitude, then one obtains a smooth curve with two humps situated about twenty degrees from the dip equator. This is the equatorial anomaly (fig. 5.6). It is anomalous because one would expect the greatest electron concentrations, and hence the highest critical frequencies, at places where the sun is highest in the sky. In other words, at the Equator.

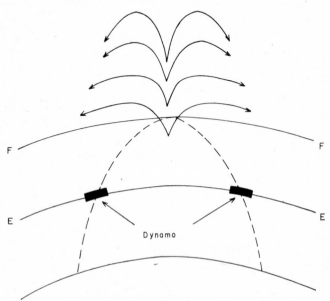

Fig. 5.7. The Fountain effect. Electric fields produced in the dynamo region travel along the Earth's magnetic field lines, which are equipotentials, to the F region. Then a combination of $\mathbf{E} \times \mathbf{B}$ drifts and diffusion produces a decreased concentration of ionization at the Equator and enhanced concentrations on each side of the Equator.

The existence of the equatorial anomaly depends on the fact that magnetic field lines are good conductors. This has two consequences:

Firstly, electrons can easily diffuse along the magnetic field lines. Since the greatest production of electrons occurs at the Equator, the greatest diffusion will be away from the Equator.

Secondly, an electric field generated in the dynamo region travels up the highly conducting field lines and appears undiminished in the F region. Because of this, the F region is permeated by horizontal electric fields generated in the E region and these electric fields produce vertical $\mathbf{E} \times \mathbf{B}$ drifts of the ionization. Since E region

102

electric fields are westward at low latitudes during the day, the resulting drift will be upwards.

These two effects, diffusion and $\mathbf{E} \times \mathbf{B}$ drifts produce an overall motion of the ionization that is upwards and away from the dip equator. This mechanism resembles the workings of a fountain, so that this explanation of the equatorial anomaly is known as the fountain effect (fig. 5.7). The presence of a meridional (north–south) wind produces an asymmetrical distribution for the anomaly.

Certain airglow emissions, known as tropical arcs, also show an equatorial anomaly. They are much brighter twenty degrees from the dip equator than at the dip equator itself. The airglow produced by atomic oxygen in the red part of the spectrum at 630 nm shows the equatorial anomaly very clearly. The reason for this is that the O_2^+ and O^+ concentrations follow the same distribution in latitude as electrons do. Because there are more oxygen ions at $\pm 20°$ dip latitude, the airglow intensity will be correspondingly greater.

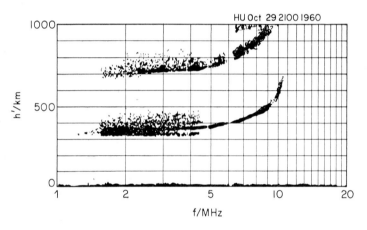

Fig. 5.8. An equatorial spread F configuration.

Spread F

Spread F has acquired its name from the diffuse spreading that sometimes occurs on the F traces of ionograms (fig. 5.8). Spread F can be divided into two types: equatorial and high latitude. Typical equatorial spread F is marked by a diffusive spreading of the ionogram trace at lower frequencies called range-spreading. It only occurs at night, and most spread F occurs just after sunset. At middle and high latitudes the width of the spread F trace increases with frequency on the ionogram and is a maximum near the critical frequency. This non-equatorial type of spread F is called frequency spreading.

103

Spread F displays all the characteristics of turbulence, yet we know that the atmosphere above 110 km has a laminar flow. This makes it extremely difficult to construct an adequate theory to explain it, though there are various competing alternatives. Because the whole of the bottom F region is turbulent during spread F it completely disrupts trans-equatorial radio propagation. This was especially noticeable on the Singapore to London teletype link, which ceased sending signals to Singapore for two or three hours out of every twenty-four during periods of high solar activity. Before the reason for this was known, operators at Singapore attributed the complete breakdown in communication in either direction to the inefficiency of the staff at the receiving end, and they referred to the lull in traffic as the ' London lunchtime effect '.

The presence of equatorial spread F also means that radio astronomy is impractical near the magnetic equator. As soon as spread F occurs, the radio signal from a star scintillates violently and no useful information can be recorded. Scintillation is the word we use to describe twinkling in the radio wave spectrum. Optical stars twinkle because of the local heating in the troposphere. Radio stars scintillate because of the turbulence in the thermosphere. Both phenomena are a curse to the astronomer.

5.6. *The polar ionosphere*

The behaviour of the high-latitude ionosphere is very complicated. There are a number of reasons for this. Solar heating of the polar regions is unique—six months of sunshine ($\chi < 90°$) and six months of darkness ($\chi > 90°$). The magnetic field lines are vertical, encouraging vertical diffusion. The magnetic field lines on the Earth's night-time side are ' open '—that is, they are elongated into the magnetospheric tail and do not necessarily meet near the South Pole (fig. 1.7). And finally, high energy particles from the solar wind and from the Van Allen belts travel along magnetic field lines and bombard the polar ionosphere.

The nature of the polar ionosphere is inseparable from the behaviour of the magnetosphere because of their link through magnetic field lines. Because of this, certain characteristic features of the polar ionosphere which could have been included in this section will be discussed in the next chapter on the magnetosphere. I will restrict myself in this section to dealing with some of the unusual properties of the high latitude ionosphere.

The disturbed ionosphere

Disturbances in the upper atmosphere follow upon major disturbances on the Sun and can be separated into those due to X-radiation and those produced by actual particles emitted by the disturbed region of the Sun. This latter type of disturbance is, in general, very complicated, since the protons and electrons that are involved have unusual trajectories because of their interaction with the solar and terrestrial magnetic fields. They will be touched upon in the next chapter.

Sudden ionospheric disturbances due to X-rays from the Sun follow the solar disturbance almost immediately. Three or four hours later highly energetic protons, with energies in the MeV range, penetrate the polar atmosphere down to D region heights and produce severe radio wave absorption known as polar cap absorption (PCA). Twenty or thirty hours later the less energetic particles arrive and indirectly produce ionospheric storms which result in high-latitude spread F, sporadic E and aurora.

Polar cap absorption (PCA)

Consider a flux of energetic charged particles coming towards the Earth. While they are still at some distance from the Earth, the particles begin to deviate from their original paths because of the influence of the geomagnetic field. The problem of the motion of a charged particle in the geomagnetic field is a difficult and complex one. It can be simplified by approximating the geomagnetic field by that of a dipole, and in this form it was first attacked by Störmer (1874–1957), a Norwegian theoretical physicist.

Störmer's theory showed that there is a cut-off energy at each parallel of magnetic latitude, such that particles with less energy than the cut-off energy cannot reach the Earth at vertical incidence. The relationship between the cut-off energy for protons and magnetic latitude is shown in fig. 5.9.

Half the total energy of a proton is lost in the last 2·5 km of its path. It loses this energy by collisions of such force that the air becomes ionized and hence the ionization produced by the proton will be greatly concentrated near the end of its track, since that is where most of the energy is lost. The increased ionization produced by the proton is then responsible for increased radio absorption because the absorption coefficient for radio waves increases as N does. (Section 4.4 gives a mathematical expression for the absorption coefficient: it is directly proportional to N.) Protons with energies in the neighbourhood of 100 MeV have the maximum efficiency for producing 30 MHz radio wave absorption. This efficiency drops very rapidly for proton energies less than 30 MeV and drops rather slowly for proton energies greater than 200 MeV.

We can now see why absorption events initiated by energetic solar particles are confined to the poles. The energy of these particles is so great that they can easily burst through the magnetopause, and are deflected by the parts of the Earth's magnetic field that are very much like a dipole. By using fig. 5.9 we see that a 100 MeV proton will only penetrate the atmosphere at magnetic latitudes greater than 65°.

Sometimes the particles responsible for the PCA do not appear to have come from the Sun by the most direct route. In one experiment in which equipment aboard a satellite was used to record the times at which particles of different speeds arrived, the results were consistent with the idea that all the particles had been emitted simultaneously from the Sun and had travelled the same distance, the fastest arriving first, but the distance they had travelled was considerably greater than the Sun–Earth distance. This experiment confirmed other indirect evidence, based on a comparison between travel times and penetration depths into the ionosphere, that showed that the route taken by the particles from the Sun to the Earth was often a round-about one.

One suggested explanation is that the protons emerge from the Sun in a direction that would not lead them to impinge on the Earth, but during their travel they are deviated towards the Earth by encountering irregularities in the interplanetary magnetic field that travels with the solar wind. Another suggestion is that the rapidly moving particles

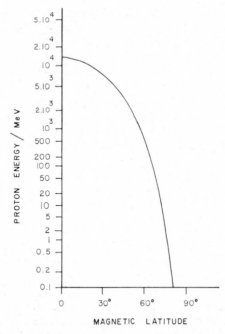

Fig. 5.9. Cut-off energy as a function of geomagnetic latitude for vertically incident protons. The Earth's magnetic field is assumed to be that of a dipole. (1 MeV = $1 \cdot 6 \times 10^{-13}$ J.)

106

are trapped in a distorted portion of the interplanetary magnetic field moving away from the Sun with a speed less than that of the individual particles. This situation has been described by saying that the rapidly moving particles are trapped, like flies, in a magnetic bottle (fig. 5.10) which moves towards the Earth, the speed of the bottle determines the time between the flare and the PCA, whereas the speed of the individual particles determines how far they can penetrate into the ionosphere.

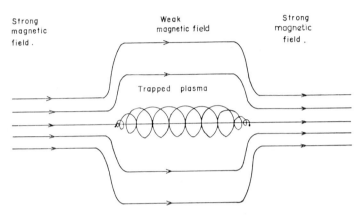

Fig. 5.10. A magnetic bottle. The gyrating trapped plasma bounces backwards and forwards between its mirror points.

The undisturbed ionosphere

The existence of the ionosphere during the polar winter when no radiation is shining on it, is yet another anomaly that has to be explained. The peak of the F layer, in fact, behaves as if radiation were still arriving. Thus, at the time when the Sun is most nearly rising (what would be midday if it did rise) the electron concentration is greatest, and at times when it is furthest from rising (corresponding to midnight) the concentration is least.

There seem to be two effects that have to be taken into account in order to explain this anomaly. Firstly, the neutral air winds blow across the polar regions from the day hemisphere towards the night hemisphere (fig. 3.9). Since the charged particles are constrained to move along the magnetic field lines, the neutral air winds produce vertical drifts in the F region which affect both the height and concentration of the F layer peak in a twenty-four hour cycle. Secondly, there seems to be a frequent input of electrons from the van Allen belts to the polar ionosphere. This input of electrons is related to the solar activity and during winter it is the main mechanism guaranteeing the existence of the polar ionosphere.

107

Further reading:

Bates, D. R., 1973. The normal E and F layers, *Journal of Atmospheric and Terrestrial Physics*, **35,** 1935–1952.

Beynon, W. J. G., 1974, Incoherent scatter sounding of the ionosphere, *Contemporary Physics*, **15,** 329–352.

Beer, Tom, 1973. The equatorial ionosphere, *Contemporary Physics*, **14,** 319–327.

Rishbeth, Henry, 1973. Physics and chemistry of the ionosphere, *Contemporary Physics*, **14,** 229–249.

The above four articles are written at the same level as this chapter. The major textbooks on ionospheric physics, all written at about 4th year university level are:

Ratcliffe, J. A., 1972. *An Introduction to the Ionosphere and Magnetosphere.* (Cambridge University Press.)

Rishbeth, Henry, and Garriott, Owen K., 1969. *Introduction to Ionospheric Physics.* (New York and London: Academic Press.)

Whitten, R. C., and Poppoff, I. G., 1971. *Fundamentals of Aeronomy.* (New York: John Wiley.)

the magnetosphere

6.1. *The exosphere*

THE exosphere is the uppermost region of the atmosphere where collisions between molecules are so infrequent that neutral particles move in trajectories subject only to gravity, whereas the ionized particles are constrained by the magnetic field. The base of the exosphere is at 600 km altitude.

Any particle entering the exosphere from below will have a certain upward velocity that is appropriate to the gas temperature. It will continue to move upwards until it either escapes from the Earth or re-enters the atmosphere from above. If a particle is to escape from the Earth's gravitational field it must have a kinetic energy greater than the gravitational potential energy at the radial distance r_e of the lower boundary of the exosphere (measured from the centre of the Earth). So, if m is the mass of the particle and v_e its velocity then it will escape if $\frac{1}{2}mv_e^2 > mg_e r_e$ where g_e is the acceleration due to gravity at the bottom of the exosphere. The escape velocity, v_e, is then given by

$$v_e = \sqrt{(2g_e r_e)} = 11\cdot4 \text{ km s}^{-1},$$

It is independent of the particle's mass.

In the thermosphere, gas particles have a Maxwellian distribution of velocities and when they move into the exosphere those with the greatest velocities can escape. For a given temperature, the lightest atoms will have the highest velocities. The velocity of hydrogen atoms is sufficiently near the escape velocity for an important number to leave the top of the atmosphere; for helium atoms the number is very much less, but can be important especially when the temperature is great. For oxygen the number is never important and heavier gases hardly escape at all.

Because atomic hydrogen is the lightest element it has the greatest scale height. The diminution of hydrogen as one ascends is less than the decrease in the amount of helium, nitrogen or oxygen as they are all heavier. At the greatest heights atomic hydrogen is the main constituent of the atmosphere. But, as we have just seen, a certain portion of the hydrogen is always escaping from the top.

If both hydrogen and helium are escaping out of the top of the atmosphere, why is it that we do not find any significant decrease in the total amount of hydrogen and helium in the atmosphere? The reason seems to be that there are sources that produce both these gases at just the right rate to balance their loss. Hydrogen is being replenished by photochemical dissociation of water vapour near the turbopause. Helium is one of the end products of the decay of radioactive rocks on the Earth. Both hydrogen and helium move upward through the atmosphere at a rate controlled by diffusion. The precise concentration of the gases depends markedly on the temperature, and especially on the thermospheric temperature, since temperature controls both the escape rate and the rate of diffusion through the other gases.

We know that the limiting thermospheric temperature is independent of altitude and this is true in the exosphere as well. The limiting thermospheric temperature, sometimes written T_∞, is the exospheric temperature. The calculated height distributions of the important gases are drawn, for three different values of T_∞, in fig. 6.1. It is noticeable that, because scale height is proportional to temperature, the concentration at great heights is greater when the temperature is greater, for all gases except hydrogen. For hydrogen, however, the concentration is smaller when the temperature is greater, because then the rate of diffusion upwards, and the rate of escape at the top, are greater.

The polar wind and the plasmapause

There is no doubt that at night hydrogen and helium will escape in the manner described above. During the daytime the picture is more complicated because most hydrogen and helium atoms that have velocities above the escape velocity are ionized as they attempt to leave the exosphere. As soon as this happens the H^+ and He^+ ions can no longer move freely but are forced to follow the magnetic field lines which, in most cases, deliver them back to the exosphere in the opposite hemisphere.

When we think about exospheric and magnetospheric motions along field lines then we need to be aware that there are two types of magnetospheric field lines: closed and open. You can see the difference in fig. 6.2 and in fig. 1.7. Closed field lines have both their ends terminating on the Earth's surface. Open field lines have one end at the Earth and one end in interplanetary space. Open field lines are only found at high latitudes on the Earth's surface. However, you can find open field lines at any latitude if you are willing to travel high enough. For example, if we travel upwards away from the magnetic equator at night, we will continually meet closed field lines until we reach a height of three Earth radii. From then on all the terrestrial

110

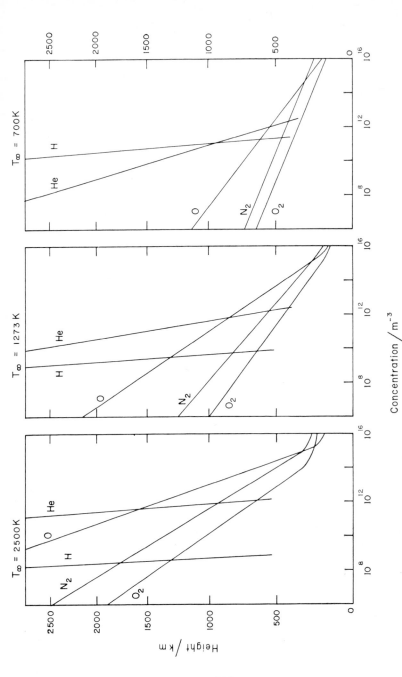

Fig. 6.1. Concentrations of the principal exospheric gases for high, medium and low exospheric temperatures. The height scale is adjusted so that the plots are straight lines in spite of the fact that the scale heights are increasing as g decreases with height.

111

magnetic field lines are open. Processes occurring on the Earth at high latitudes can also be important at sufficient heights above low latitude points.

In the high latitude polar regions, however, the H⁺ and He⁺ can still escape at night. This is because the nightside high latitude magnetic field lines are open. Once a hydrogen or helium particle has reached escape velocity then it will keep going, quickly become ionized and follow the open magnetic field lines to the depths of space behind the Earth (fig. 6.2). The resulting movement of plasma away from the high latitude regions is called the polar wind.

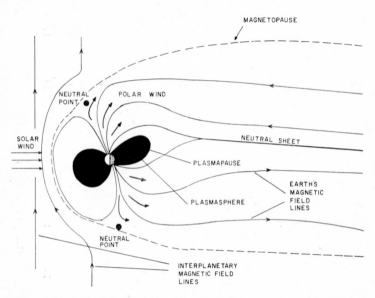

Fig. 6.2. The drift of H⁺ and He⁺ from high altitudes causes the polar wind. This depletes the polar exosphere producing a sharp plasmapause where the plasma concentration increases. Neutral points, where there is no magnetic field are also shown when the interplanetary magnetic field has a northward component.

The loss of charged particles caused by the polar wind seriously depletes the high latitude exosphere of ions and electrons. This shows up markedly on experiments conducted from satellites that are designed to measure the magnetospheric electron density profile. As we can see in fig. 6.3, there is a sharp kink in the electron density profile over the equator at four Earth radii from the Earth's centre. This kink is known as Carpenter's knee after its discoverer, and it marks the location of the plasmapause (fig. 6.2). Above the plasmapause the electron density is depleted to about 10^7 m⁻³ because of the polar wind. Below the plasmapause lies the plasmasphere, the region in which the plasma concentration is around 10^{10} m^{-3}.

The plasmapause then is demarcated by the magnetic field line that rises four Earth radii above the Earth's centre at the Equator. In shortened form this is known as the $L = 4$ field line. The magnetic field line that rises to seven Earth radii above the Earth's centre at the dip equator is the $L = 7$ line, and so on. Notice that $L = 7$ rises to only six Earth radii above the Earth's *surface*.

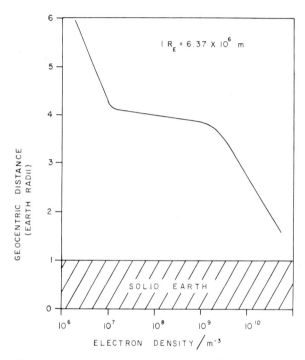

Fig. 6.3. The electron concentration as a function of geocentric distance above the Equator. The sharp gradient at three Earth radii above the Earth's surface is the plasmapause. Because of the shape of this profile the plasmapause is often called Carpenter's knee, after its discoverer.

If we examine the $L = 4$ field line then we are examining the plasmapause. Maps of the Earth's magnetic field reveal that the $L = 4$ line is at an altitude of 2000 km at a geographic latitude of 55°N, at 1000 km altitude at 57°N and at 100 km altitude at 60°N. This means that at around fifty-five degrees geographic latitude the plasmapause is in the F region and it is almost vertical. If a satellite takes topside soundings between 55°N and 60°N there will be a sudden decrease in the electron density at 1000 km altitude. The sudden minimum in electron density as one moves north in the northern hemisphere has been called the mid-latitude trough.

Radiation belts

The particles that go to make up the plasmasphere have energies of the order of 0·1 eV, corresponding to electron temperatures of a few thousand degrees. We have just seen that there are 10^9 to 10^{10} of these particles per cubic metre near the plasmapause. Coexistent with these low energy particles are very large energy particles, with energies in the keV to MeV range. There are not very many of these high energy particles, their concentration is only about 10^4 m^{-3}, but because of their high energies they have energy densities of 10^7 to at least 10^{10} eV m^{-3} and so make an extremely important contribution to the energy of the magnetosphere.

Energetic charged particles in the magnetosphere eventually find their way into two stable regions where they are trapped. These are the Van Allen belts. The inner belt at a geocentric distance of 1·5 Earth radii at the Equator (or, more simply put, on the $L = 1·5$ magnetic field line) contains protons with energies of tens and hundreds of MeV. The outer belt, lying along the $L = 4$ magnetic field line (which, as we just saw, is the field line that rises to a height of four Earth radii above the Earth's centre), consists of energetic electrons from tens to keV to a few MeV. Thus the outer belt coincides with the plasmapause.

The particles trapped within the radiation belts have a complex motion that can be described as a combination of three types, which are sketched in fig. 6.4. Particles gyrate about the lines of magnetic force in circular orbits. The centre of gyration bounces back and forth along the field line between the mirror points. And the particles themselves drift in longitude eastward (electrons) or westward (ions) as shown by the hollow arrows.

The reason for the gyration of charged particles in a magnetic field was discussed in Section 1.5. For the trapped particles in the radiation belts, the gyroperiod is of the order of 10^{-6} s for electrons and 10^{-3} s, for protons, the radius of gyration being about 0·5 km and 10 km respectively.

Particles bounce backwards and forwards between the mirror points in about 0·5 s. The mirror points are usually high enough that collisions are extremely rare, and this is why the Van Allen belts are so stable. On the rare occasion that a collision does take place the particle loses its energy, moves into the lower ionosphere and becomes indistinguishable from all the other low energy particles in the plasmasphere. The depth of the mirror point depends on the closeness of the turns in the helical path as the particle crosses the Equator,

114

where the geomagnetic field is horizontal. This closeness is measured in terms of the pitch angle (α) between the magnetic field and the particle's velcoity.

The existence of mirror points arises from the dipole nature of the Earth's magnetic field in the Van Allen belt regions. Because the magnetic field is stronger at lower heights there is a bunching of magnetic field lines near polar areas. This bunching of field lines acts like a magnetic bottle (fig. 5.10) and traps the plasma within it. A particle crossing the dip equator (where the magnetic field is B_0) with a pitch angle α follows a field line down towards the Earth until the field strength reaches a magnitude B_m such that $\sin^2 \alpha = B_0/B_m$; the motion along the field line then ceases momentarily, the mirror point has been reached, and the particle returns along its path. The depth of the mirror point does not depend on the nature of the particle or on its energy but only on the pitch angle of its motion and the shape of the magnetic field.

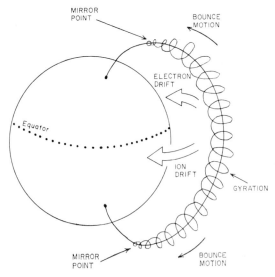

Fig. 6.4. Sketch of the motion of energetic particles trapped on a magneto-spheric field line. The total motion is made up of three parts: gyrations, bounces and drifts.

The helical motion of the particles bouncing between their mirror points drifts slowly sideways around the Earth, towards the east for electrons and towards the west for protons. This east–west drift of the trapped particles occurs because the Earth's dipole field decreases in strength upwards. A gyrating particle has a larger radius of gyration at the top of its trajectory than at the bottom so that it drifts sideways (fig. 6.5). The time for a complete revolution about the Earth depends on the height and on the energy of the particles, but typical times for electrons are 50 min and for protons 30 min.

The oppositely directed drifts of the protons and electrons around the Earth constitutes a current, called the ring current. Since all currents, by convention, flow in the direction that the positive charged particles move, the ring current flows westward. The ring current produces a small magnetic field near the surface of the Earth. This field points southward so that it slightly decreases the magnetic field at the Earth's surface. By monitoring the small sudden changes in the overall magnetic field at the Earth's surface, we can detect any sudden increase or decrease in the number of trapped particles in the Van Allen belts.

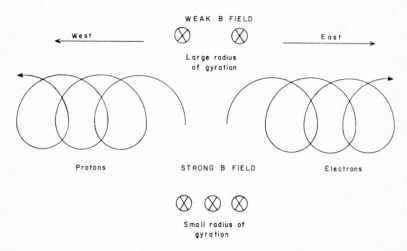

Fig. 6.5. The east–west drift of trapped energetic particles occurs because the Earth's magnetic field decreases in strength upwards. A gyrating particle moves in a larger circle at the top of its orbit than at the bottom. This diagram is drawn looking northward so that the field is directed into the paper.

There appear to be two important sources for protons and electrons in the radiation belts. The first is the neutron albedo* method of charged particle generation. A galactic cosmic ray penetrating deeply into the atmosphere causes a nuclear disintegration and liberates a neutron which then travels into the magnetosphere and

---

* This should not be confused with the planetary albedo, which is an astronomical term referring to the proportion of incident sunlight reflected from a planet's surface.

decays to produce an electron and a proton (fig. 6.6). The decay process is

$$n \rightarrow p^+ + e^- + \bar{\nu} + 780 \text{ keV}.$$

About 500 keV of the energy liberated is taken by the chargeless, almost massless neutrino ($\bar{\nu}$), which then travels back out to space with it. This leaves about 300 keV of the neutron's mass, almost all of which goes to the electron. Both the proton and the electron also start life with a velocity (v) equal to that of the neutron, so that each has a kinetic energy of $\frac{1}{2}mv^2$. Because of the small mass of the electrons this extra energy is negligible compared with the 300 keV it got from the nuclear disintegration of the neutron's rest mass. For a proton the kinetic energy is more important than the disintegration energy, so that its final energy may be of the order of 10 MeV.

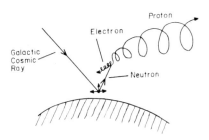

Fig. 6.6. The neutron albedo mechanism. A neutron 'backsplashed' after its formation travels into the exosphere then decays to form an electron–proton pair. Both the 300 keV electron and 10 MeV proton can become trapped in the Earth's magnetic field.

The second major source for the Van Allen belt particles seems to be the magnetospheric tail. Low-energy particles already present in other parts of the magnetosphere are accelerated to the radiation belts where they are trapped. Some of these accelerated particles are not completely trapped and manage to fall on the polar ionosphere where they produce aurorae. (See the region in fig. 1.7, p. 15, marked as quasi-trapped particles.)

6.2. Storms

Observations of the interplanetary magnetic field, which is being shot out from the sun, reveal that it points towards the Sun or away from the Sun. To someone on the Earth's equator, this means that at noon the interplanetary field is either straight up or straight down. There are also small east–west and north–south components of the field. The north–south component, though only a small part of the total interplanetary magnetic field is very important. Normally it points northward and then the magnetosphere is as shown in fig. 6.2. When it points southward, all hell breaks loose (fig. 6.7). There are changes in the Earth's magnetic field called magnetic storms, there are changes in the ionosphere called ionospheric storms and there is an increase in the number and the intensity of aurorae. Frequently, the magnetic field reversal is also accompanied by an enhancement of the solar wind in both speed and concentration. Then the storm effects are even stronger.

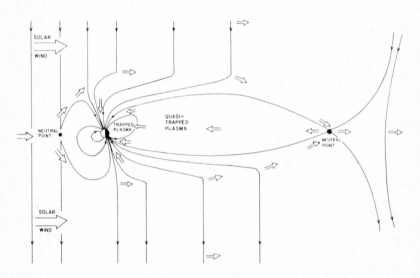

Fig. 6.7. The interaction of the geomagnetic field with the interplanetary magnetic field when it has a southward component. The plasma moves with, and along, the interplanetary magnetic field as it moves away from the Sun. The plasma motion is shown by hollow arrows. It is injected into the magnetosphere directly at the poles or indirectly via the tail. Compare this with fig. 6.2.

When the interplanetary magnetic field has a southward component then it manages to connect with the Earth's magnetic field. Because the solar wind plasma is strung out along the interplanetary magnetic field lines as it moves through space, there are now two ways in which the solar plasma can penetrate into the magnetosphere. It can slide straight down a field line or it can come in through the tail.

It is possible to differentiate between particles arriving directly and those coming via the tail. The solar wind near the Earth has a temperature of half a million to one million kelvins. This temperature corresponds to particle energies of $\frac{3}{2}kT$, which upon

118

evaluation range from 75 eV to 150 eV. Charged particles of this energy striking the neutral atmosphere produces displays of the aurora in the form of a red emission at 630·0 nm. The particles coming in from the neutral point* in the magnetospheric tail are accelerated towards the Earth and through this acceleration they acquire energies up to a few MeV. The exact mechanism that produces this acceleration is still not known and this remains one of the major problems of magnetospheric physics.

We can be pretty certain that the acceleration towards the Earth has to be produced by an electric field, but how does the electric field get there? Many theoreticians, and even more experimentalists, when faced with this problem loosely wave their hands and say: " Oh, plasma instabilities set up the fields ". What they mean by this is that because of the configuration of the plasma some electrons and ions separate, produce an electric field and that this electric field, which drives the rest of the plasma, grows and grows and is unstable. This may well be true, but as yet no one has shown that this is really what is happening.

Some of these accelerated particles become fully trapped in the Van Allen radiation belts. The rest remain in a quasi-trapped state, wandering around the magnetospheric tail until they escape again or are dumped at the poles to produce an aurora. Since these particles are more energetic, the resulting aurora will also appear more energetic, having a violent dancing motion.

We know that the solar wind plasma is so energetic that it carries the solar magnetic field along with it and this is the reason that the interplanetary magnetic field lines, which are said to be frozen to the plasma, move from the left to the right of fig. 6.7. But since these solar magnetic field lines are attached to the geomagnetic field lines, they drag the geomagnetic field lines along with them producing magnetospheric convection. Since the ions and electrons in the upper ionosphere and magnetosphere have to stay along the geomagnetic field lines they also convect, adding slightly to the polar wind. New geomagnetic field lines then form on the dayside and are in turn convected to the nightside of the Earth. At their base these field lines are attached to the highly conducting dynamo region at 100 km. (Remember: a good conductor has no fields within it and all fields emanate from it at right angles.) Thus, the particles moving at the base of the geomagnetic field lines set up a current in the high latitude dynamo region—the polar current.

* A neutral point is a point in the magnetosphere where the magnetic flux density is zero. There are two neutral points whose location depends on the north–south orientation of the interplanetary magnetic field (see figs. 6.2 and 6.7). They should not be confused with the neutral sheet depicted in fig. 6.2.

Aurorae

The most beautiful and most impressive manifestation of the workings of the upper atmosphere can be seen in the polar aurora. Only direct observations can reveal its three-dimensional grandeur, but some of the beauty can be captured in photographs such as fig. 6.8. The structure of quiet aurorae as in this figure, consists of one or more thin arcs stretching east to west from horizon to horizon. These quiet aurorae are caused by the quasi-trapped particles in the magnetosphere randomly dribbling into the polar atmosphere during periods when the interplanetary magnetic field points northward. Periodically the quiet arcs break up in a burst of activity associated with magnetic and ionospheric storms. They then brighten and spread across the sky, to be followed by a gradual return to their quiet forms.

The fact that it is energetic particles, such as protons and electrons, impinging on the polar region that causes aurorae has long been suspected. The first suggestions along these lines were made when the glow from the newly discovered cathode ray tube was compared to the aurora. The similarities were striking. The most common colour in cathode ray tubes filled with air, and in aurorae, is green, both because the maximum response of the human eyes occurs in the green and, in the case of the aurora, because of the strong emission at 557·7 nm from atomic oxygen at altitudes of 100 to 150 km. Aurorae are seen as green, white, red, blue and yellow in order of increasing rarity.

During magnetospheric storms, when the interplanetary magnetic field has a southward component, we have seen how particles arrive at the poles along two completely different routes. The particles sliding directly down the connected field lines produce Type A aurorae. The electrons with energies of about 100 eV produce a characteristic red emission at 630·0 nm in the 150 km to 400 km height range. The particles that have been accelerated to the polar regions from the magnetospheric tail produce Type B aurorae. Molecular emissions, excited by energetic electrons up to 10 keV and above, show up in a variety of colours—often appearing white in their totality. The energetic particles of Type B aurorae can penetrate the atmosphere to lower heights and these aurorae extend upwards from as low as 85 km.

It has been found that during auroral displays radio waves can be reflected by the aurora. Since this was also found to happen when there was no aurora visible, this effect was called radio aurora—to distinguish it from visual aurora. The two are almost certainly the same thing; it is just that at times it is possible to ionize the atmosphere without emitting visible light. This is especially true during the daytime. Daytime radio aurorae provided the first clue as to the

Fig. 6.8.   Auroral display.   (Photograph by G. Lamprecht.)

presence of daytime aurorae. Nowadays, by using sensitive optical detectors both daytime aurorae and faint night-time aurorae can be detected. At the very lowest thresholds of visibility it becomes difficult to differentiate between faint aurora (which is produced by collisions with electrons and protons) and bright airglow (which is produced by chemical reactions started by solar radiation) but in a bright aurora there is no difficulty.

Visual aurorae generally occur along an oval situated between 60° and 80° magnetic latitudes (fig. 6.9), though during exceptionally strong storms the auroral oval can extend down to 50°. The auroral oval was first discovered by observations from the ground made well before the existence of the magnetosphere was known. It was originally a very puzzling feature of aurorae but we can now easily explain it. The precipitating particles that cause the aurorae must travel to the polar regions along magnetic field lines, so that the auroral oval must represent the intersection of the upper atmosphere with the quasi-trapped region of the magnetosphere from which the auroral particles come. We know that the magnetosphere is distorted by the solar wind so that the field lines are closer to the magnetic pole on the daytime side and further on the night-time side. Hence the auroral oval.

The auroral oval stays fixed in position while the Earth rotates under it. Any place inside the hatched areas of fig. 6.9 will see auroral displays whereas those places not in the hatched areas will not. But as the Earth rotates, new areas move into the auroral oval and some areas leave the auroral oval. When many auroral displays are analysed statistically, the most common occurrence is in a zone that is occupied in succession by the night portions of these ovals. This auroral zone is roughly circular around the geomagnetic pole.

During magnetospheric storms there is a sudden influx of particles to the magnetospheric tail. Not only does this alter the type of aurora that is visible but it extends both the auroral oval and the auroral zone. We do not know how far the auroral zone can extend altogether if a super-strong magnetospheric storm occurs. One of my colleagues has pointed out to me that there is a record in the national archives of an auroral observation in Ghana (or the Gold Coast as it was then called) on 17 November, 1924. Can aurorae really be seen that far south (or if one is thinking of aurora australis—the southern lights—that far north)? I doubt it.* There is no record of any unusual solar activity or magnetic activity that would have warranted an exceptionally strong aurora. Most probably the observer mistook some other natural phenomenon for the aurora.

* The only observation of an aurora in the tropics of which I am aware occurred during the severe magnetic storm of February 4, 1872 when a vivid aurora was seen from Bombay.

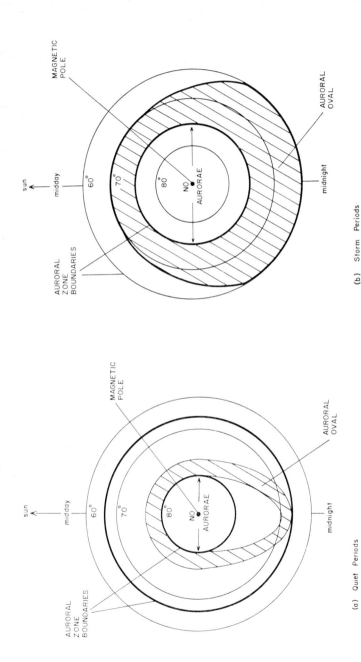

(a) Quiet Periods

(b) Storm Periods

Fig. 6.9. During an auroral display the aurorae are found to be located inside the hatched area, called the auroral oval. As the Earth rotates beneath the oval, new locations get to see the aurorae. All the locations on the surface of the Earth that can see the aurorae lie within a circular auroral zone. The locations of the auroral oval and zone are shown for (a) quiet periods and (b) storm periods.

123

Magnetic storms

The changes in the magnetosphere during a storm can be monitored by watching the small changes in the magnitude of the Earth's magnetic field. Since these changes are at the most only 2% of the background field, sensitive magnetometers have to be used.

The first indication of a storm on the magnetic records is a sudden jump of about 20 nT (1 nT is often called a gamma, γ) in the magnetic field strength (fig. 6.10). This is the sudden commencement of the storm. It is due to the arrival of an enhanced solar wind at the boundary of the magnetosphere. The enhanced solar wind increases the compression of the magnetic field lines already caused by the normal wind. This compression increases the magnetic field strength.

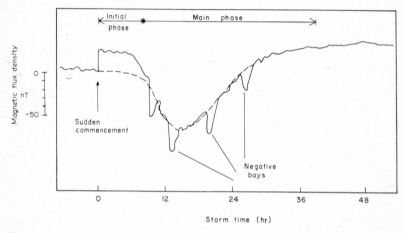

Fig. 6.10. Schematic magnetogram showing the storm variations of the geomagnetic field. The broken line shows the variation of the ring current caused by extra particles in the Van Allen belts.

The sudden arrival of the enhanced solar wind has the form of a shock wave; it is followed by a more-or-less steady enhanced solar wind that results in a continuing compression of the field lines. The corresponding increase of field at the surface of the Earth is called the initial phase of the storm.

The onset of a storm is not necessarily marked by an enhanced solar wind, though in most cases it is, and occasionally there may not be a sudden commencement. Then the magnetic field variation follows the dotted line of fig. 6.10, which is due to the enhanced ring current. About 6 to 10 hours after the beginning of a magnetospheric storm, there is an increase in the number of energetic particles in the radiation belts. These are the solar wind particles that have arrived via the magnetospheric tail. As these more numerous energetic particles drift in their trapped motion around the Earth, electrons eastward and protons westward, they produce an increased ring current. Since the westward ring current produces a southward magnetic field, an increased ring current produces a decrease in the magnetic field at the ground. This decrease is called the main phase of the magnetic storm. After new particles cease to be injected the ring current slowly decays for one or two days, and the magnetic field gradually returns to its normal value: this is the recovery phase of the storm. If there is an enhanced solar wind but the interplanetary magnetic field does not have a southward component the main phase will be missing. There will be only an initial phase and nothing else.

The main phase of a magnetic storm is often interspersed with magnetic bays, which are rather abrupt disturbances lasting an hour or two, and which can be positive or negative. Four large negative bays are shown in fig. 6.10 (they are called bays because of their shape.) Magnetic bays are related to the magnetospheric field lines' connection with the interplanetary magnetic lines and the subsequent magnetospheric convection. The movement of the electrons in the high-latitude dynamo region following these field lines produces the polar current system. The number of electrons in the polar dynamo region fluctuates depending on the number of particles from the solar wind sliding down the field lines. These fluctuations then show up as the bays.

Ionospheric storms

Magnetospheric storms have their ultimate cause in increased solar activity. Ionospheric effects of the solar activity show up as soon as the enhanced radiation from the Sun reaches the Earth. The onset of a sudden ionospheric disturbance is the first warning that a severe magnetospheric storm is brewing.

Next comes polar cap absorption. This time a result of the faster and more energetic particles from the Sun. Lastly come the auroral and magnetic disturbances detailed above.

The increased ultraviolet radiation during a storm increases the ionospheric temperature which controls most of the chemistry of the ionosphere. This in turn produces changes in the F region, decreasing the electron concentration over most of the world.

6.3. *Conjugate effects*

We know that many effects observed on the Earth such as aurorae, magnetic storms, etc., are in some way a reflection of solar activity. Conjugate point studies are an extra method of determining the links in the chain of events that begin with a disturbance on the Sun.

The effects of certain upper atmospheric or magnetospheric disturbances can propagate along magnetic field lines. The propagation can be by particles, by electromagnetic waves or by fields. If the points on the Earth where the information is measured or observed are linked by a common geomagnetic field line, then these are referred to as conjugate points. Some conjugate points, along with their L values, are listed in Table 6.1.

Conjugate points	L value
Frobisher Bay, Canada—South Pole	14·17
Great Whale River, Canada—Byrd Station, Antarctica	7·12
Kotzebue, Alaska—Macquarie Is.	5·23
Quebec City, Canada—Eights Station, Antarctica	3·92
Cold Bay, Alaska—Oamaru, New Zealand	2·65
Valencia, Spain—Capetown, South Africa	1·75
San Juan, Puerto Rico—Trelew, Argentina	1·39
Tamale, Ghana—Tamale, Ghana	1·00

Table 6.1. Some conjugate points. L is the maximum extension, in Earth radii, of the magnetic field line from the Earth's centre.

The magnetosphere contains a certain number of open field lines that are swept back by the solar wind. These complicate both the determination of the positions of conjugate points and also the interpretation of conjugate events. At high latitudes, events that occur during the daytime may be conjugate, only to cease being conjugate when night falls and the field lines open.

Since most, but not all, aurorae are caused by particles precipitating from the quasi-trapped region of the magnetosphere we would expect most, but not all, aurorae to be conjugate. This was conclusively confirmed by flying two aeroplanes simultaneously at conjugate points. Both planes were equipped with all-sky cameras that took pictures of the whole sky. Not only were almost all the aurorae occurring simultaneously in both hemispheres, but much of the detailed structure of the aurora was faithfully reproduced in both locations. Let us now discuss some other phenomena found to occur at conjugate points.

Whistlers
From the earliest days of radio experimentation, various kinds of very-low frequency electromagnetic radiation have intrigued those who heard the strange mixture of glissandi whistles, hisses, chirps and warbling sounds on their headphones. The observational

126

equipment required to hear these sounds is remarkably simple. A set of headphones connected to an amplifier using a long length of telephone wire as an aerial will generally suffice.

Whistlers consist of bursts of radiation beginning at high frequency and gliding down to a few hundred hertz in a period of about one second; they originate with lightning strokes in the atmosphere and propagate between magnetically conjugate points by following the magnetic field lines.

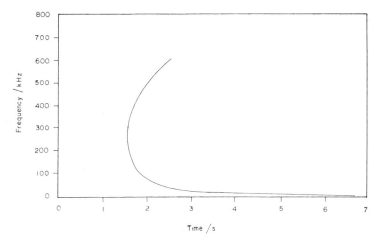

Fig. 6.11. Full sonogram of a whistler. Since the audible range does not extend above 20 kHz, the only part of the sonogram that can actually be heard is the descending tail of the whistler. Because of the shape of this curve, the phenomenon is called a nose whistler.

A lightning stroke is a short, sharp pulse of electricity. By Fourier analysing a short, sharp pulse, one finds that a lightning stroke produces electromagnetic radiation at all frequencies spread over a band from about 200 Hz to over 10^7 Hz. Most of this radiation produces 'static' on the radio but the low frequency components from 200 Hz to 30 kHz can be ducted by the Earth's magnetic field lines. These waves propagate as a right-handed circularly polarized wave with phase and group velocities well below the light velocity c. The mathematics of whistler propagation is very similar to the theory outlined in Chapter 4, but for the lowest frequency whistler waves, ion motions need to be included in the equations.

The characteristic frequency drop of a whistler can be displayed on a plot of frequency against time. This is known as a sonogram, and the full sonogram of a typical whistler is shown in fig. 6.11. Because the ear cannot hear sounds above 20 kHz the sonogram of an audible whistler will consist only of the descending tail end of the curve in fig. 6.11. The frequency drop in the audible range results from the dispersion of electromagnetic waves in the magnetospheric plasma. High frequency components travel much faster than low frequency components. To differentiate between the sonogram of an audible whistler and the full sonogram, the effect observed on the full sonogram is called a nose whistler, because of the shape of the curve. An audible whistler has no nose.

Nose whistlers are an extremely useful scientific tool. If the frequency and time delay of the nose are known then it is possible to calculate the gyrofrequency and electron density at the top of the magnetic field line along which the whistler travelled. These computations on nose whistlers provided the first evidence for the existence of the plasmapause.

Sometimes trains of whistlers are observed following each other at equal time lapses but with the rate of frequency decrease less in each successive echo. The explanation is that the whistler pulse is reflected back along the magnetic field line from which it has come. Since it has travelled twice the distance when it returns, the dispersion is even greater and the consequent rate of frequency decrease is less.

Many whistlers are preceded by a sharp click that signifies the particular lightning stroke that generated the whistler; for nearby strokes the click travels directly to the observer and so does not suffer any dispersion. When no click is heard the whistler has its source in the opposite hemisphere, at the conjugate point.

Very low frequency emissions

Other kinds of very low frequency emission are often heard as well. Steady noise up to 10 kHz—called hiss, and short-lived rising whistlers—called the dawn chorus, because it sounds like birds awakening in the morning, have both been found to be conjugate phenomena. They are quite often associated with whistlers and appear to be triggered by them by means of complex wave–particle interactions in the magnetosphere.

Micropulsations

Electromagnetic waves with frequencies below 10 Hz also exist. These waves cannot be detected by normal radio apparatus because of their extremely long wavelength, but they do show up on magneto-grams because the oscillating magnetic field of the wave interferes with the steady magnetic field of the Earth. The waves show up as small variations of about 0·5 nT in the Earth's magnetic field called micropulsations with characteristic periods ranging from a few tenths of a second to a few minutes. Experimental and theoretical investigations of the micropulsations have led to the belief that they have their origin well above the ionosphere, either in or beyond the magnetosphere. There appear in fact to be two sources generating micropulsations; the dominant source is the action of the solar wind on the magnetospheric boundary. This sets up Alfvén waves which show up as micropulsations. Oscillations of the magnetosphere with the whole cavity pulsating inwards and outwards are the second way in which micropulsations are generated.

Notation	Period range(s)
Pc 1	0·2–5
Pc 2	5–10
Pc 3	10–45
Pc 4	45–150
Pc 5	150–600
Pi 1	1–40
Pi 2	40–150

Table 6.2. Classification scheme for micropulsations.

Micropulsations are divided into two groups. Continuous micropulsations, denoted by Pc are those which have a considerable element of continuity lasting for many hours. Irregular micropulsations, Pi, last less than an hour, and generally tend to appear during the onset of magnetic bays. Sometimes observers have even noted that the period of pulsating aurorae—when the auroral brightness waxes and wanes regularly—coincides with the Pi period. More detailed naming of the micropulsations depends on the pulsation period. The classification scheme is shown in Table 6.2. Most scientific work has concentrated on the Pc 1 pulsations which are also known as pearls. They appear like beats on magnetograms and when their sonogram is plotted the result looks like a reverse whistler; that is, their sonograms consist of a repetition of rising tones. Thus, once again, dispersion is affecting the wave but in this case in completely the opposite way to its effect on audible whistlers.

Further reading:

Roederer, Juan G., 1974. The Earth's magnetosphere, *Science*, **183**, 37–46.
Heikkila, W. J., 1973. Aurora, *Eos—the Transactions of the American Geophysical Union*, **54**, 764–768.
Beer, Tom, 1971. Particle precipitation at auroral heights, *Contemporary Physics*, **12**, 299–310.

Rothmuller, I. J., and Beer, Tom, 1972. Conjugate point phenomena, *Science Progress*, **60,** 205–215.

Sudan, R. N., and Denavit, J., 1973. VLF emissions from the magnetosphere, *Physics Today*, **26** (12), 32–39.

The books by Ratcliffe and by Rishbeth and Garriott mentioned at the end of Chapter 5 also deal with the magnetosphere. More detailed treatments will be found in:

White, R. S., 1970. *Space Physics.* (London: Gordon and Breach Science Publishers.)

Hess, W. N., 1968. *Radiation Belt and Magnetosphere.* (Waltham, Massachusetts: Blaisdell, Xerox College Publishing.)

Papagiannis, Michael, 1972. *Space Physics and Space Astronomy.* (London: Gordon and Breach Science Publishers.)

planetary aeronomy

7.1. *Introduction*

THE most exciting and rapidly changing area of present-day atmospheric research is the study of the other planets. The field is an extremely complex one to tackle because the properties of a planet's atmosphere depend upon an intricate interplay between a large number of factors. Both the planetary aeronomer and the planetary meteorologist need to call on geology, chemistry, atomic physics, fluid dynamics, electrodynamics and thermodynamics to answer their questions.

Sometimes the answer is trivial. Both Mercury and the Moon are devoid of any atmosphere, so there is nothing to study. Often the answer is more complex than we imagined. Our models for other planets are strongly influenced by our experience with the Earth. Predictions about the Martian ionosphere used to deal with an electron density of 5×10^{11} m^{-3} extending over 1000 km above the planet's surface. When the Mariner 4 spacecraft finally got there in 1965, it found an ionosphere of less than 10^{11} electrons per cubic metre squeezed into the height range 100 to 200 km above the Martian surface.

These surprising results led to important new insights in ionospheric physics and resulted in a deeper and more fundamental comprehension of the processes which shape the Earth's ionosphere.

Incidentally, only one Moon in the solar system has any significant atmosphere. It is Titan, one of the ten satellites of Saturn and the namesake of Kurt Vonnegut's novel *The Sirens of Titan*. It has a strongly hydrogen-based atmosphere with significant amounts of methane in it. The main reason that Titan can retain an atmosphere is its low temperature, which keeps velocities of the particles below their escape velocity. Hence they are trapped. Calculations show that Titan has a slightly poorer ability to hold an atmosphere than Mars.

The fundamental parameter that we need is the planet's temperature. Meteorologists are interested in the horizontal distribution of temperature, aeronomers with the vertical distribution. We saw, in Section 2.2, how to calculate the mean surface temperature of a planet. This was a good start but there was one assumption made which, though true for the Earth, needs to be checked for other planets. I assumed that the incoming radiation, which heats only one hemisphere, is re-radiated by the whole sphere.

This can be achieved in two ways—by thermal conduction or by rotation. Since the thermal conductivity of soil and stone is not high enough to distribute the temperature around a distance as great as a planetary diameter, we have to look to rotation. The question then is: does the ground or the atmosphere radiate the heat slowly enough that the temperature has not dropped appreciably before the next day begins? In scientific jargon, the radiative relaxation time has to exceed the length of the day. Pluto is the only planet in which it does not.

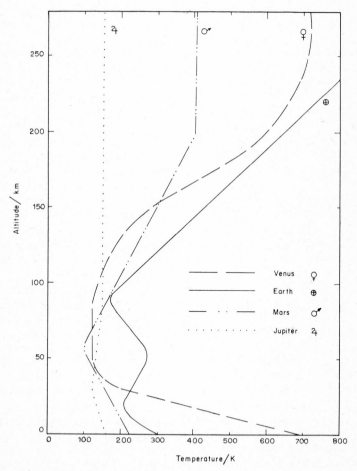

Fig. 7.1. Some typical planetary temperature distributions.

In fig. 7.1 is plotted the vertical temperature distribution for Venus, Mars and Jupiter along with the terrestrial temperature for comparison. The discussion in this chapter will be limited to these planets because we know more about their atmospheres than we do of the atmospheres of Saturn, Neptune, Uranus or Pluto.

The first point to note about fig. 7.1 is that every one of these planets has a tropopause. On Earth, the tropopause divides the lower atmosphere from the upper atmosphere and marks the height at which meteorology ceases and aeronomy starts. It is likely that the tropopause on the other planets serves a similar function.

The second point is that on all the planets the atmosphere is an exceedingly thin peel covering the planetary surface. In every planet over 90% of the atmosphere lies below 100 km. Yet 100 km is an extremely small fraction of the planetary radius; it is fifteen thousandths of the radius of the Earth—$0.015 R_E$, and it is $0.017 R_V$, $0.030 R_M$ and $0.0014 R_J$ for Venus, Mars and Jupiter respectively.

The large size of Jupiter is one of the dominating things about that planet. Jupiter, Saturn, Uranus and Neptune all have radii at least three times larger than the Earth's, whereas Venus and the Earth are roughly equal in size, and Mars is about half the size of Earth. This sudden jump in size provides a useful demarcation so that we can talk of Mercury, Venus, Earth and Mars as the inner planets and the rest as the outer planets. To emphasize the fact that Venus, Earth and Mars have atmospheres whilst Mercury does not, these three are sometimes called the terrestrial planets.

7.2. Venus

The fact that Venus has an atmosphere was discovered by the Russian poet and scientist M. V. Lomonosov (1711–1765) in 1761. However, attempts to investigate its properties during the following two centuries were not sufficiently successful for any definite results to emerge. This situation has only recently changed with the successful flights of the Soviet Venera 4, 5 and 6 and the American Mariner 5 space probes.

The lower atmosphere of Venus is 95% carbon dioxide CO_2, about 3% molecular nitrogen N_2, 1% water vapour and it has very low concentrations of HCl, H_2SO_4, HF and CO. Venus has clouds at around 50–60 km altitude, and there is no water vapour above these clouds. Both the clouds and the lower atmosphere of Venus would be very unpleasant to human beings. The mixture of H_2O and HCl is just right to produce strong hydrochloric acid drops in the clouds and hydrochloric acid vapour in the atmosphere. Venus is not the place to be when it rains!

The surface pressure of Venus is 8 MPa—eighty times the surface pressure on Earth. As we know the vertical temperature variation, and the molar mass of CO_2 (44 g mol^{-1}) we can calculate the variation of pressure and density with height by using the ideal gas equation and the barometric equation. At the same time we can calculate the expected ionosphere in a Venusian atmosphere of CO_2 by using Chapman's theory.

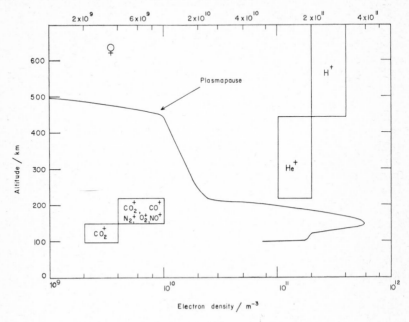

Fig. 7.2.   The daytime ionosphere of Venus.

If Venus had a pure CO_2 atmosphere with no minor constituents then the ionosphere should be a perfect single-peaked Chapman layer. The ionosphere of Venus was measured by Mariner 5 and the results are shown in fig. 7.2.   Not really like a Chapman layer at all.   This indicates that the minor constituents are affecting the chemistry of the ionosphere.   The most likely constituents responsible for the electron density profile are shown in fig. 7.2 as well, inside boxes designating their appropriate height range.

The helium content in Venus's atmosphere should far exceed its content in the Earth's atmosphere.   Due to the absence of any magnetic field, Venus has no mechanism for helium loss such as the polar wind on Earth.   Thus its He$^+$ and H$^+$ content are correspondingly greater, with the highest concentrations being on the night side of the planet.   The He$^+$ and H$^+$ ions are formed by photoionization in the day-time ionosphere and carried over to the night side by winds.

134

The He$^+$ and H$^+$ concentrations at night have been estimated at 5×10^8 ions m^{-3} of each at an altitude of 700 km.

Since Venus has no polar wind, the existence of a plasmapause at 400 km in the daytime may seem surprising. It is. During night-time the plasmapause climbs to altitudes of 4000 km so that at night, the electron concentration above 500 km is greater than during the day whereas below 500 km the opposite is true. This day–night difference in the ionosphere is due to the winds which are carrying the H$^+$ and He$^+$ ions around the planet. The day–night difference in the plasmapause height seems to suggest that the Venusian plasmapause is liable to be a manifestation of the interaction between the solar wind and the Venusian ionosphere.

7.3. Mars

Carbon dioxide is the major component of the Martian atmosphere. Both Venus and Mars have very similar compositions in the lower atmosphere, though Mars has hardly any water vapour. Mars is 95% carbon dioxide and 5% molecular nitrogen with very small traces of the minor constituents O$_2$, CO and H$_2$O. The surface pressure on the planet is 6 kPa (6×10^{-2} of the Earth's pressure).

There is still a strong controversy in progress as to the nature of the Martian upper atmosphere. One group claims that the chemistry of both Mars's and Venus's upper atmosphere is controlled by turbulent mixing and that the gases in the upper atmosphere are homogeneously mixed so that CO$_2$ predominates. The other group claims that there is chemical equilibrium in the upper atmosphere with the production and loss of all the constituents being in balance.

The argument arose because we do not know enough about the chemistry of CO$_2$. The major area of dispute centres around whether the reaction

$$CO_2^+ + e \rightarrow CO + O$$

is dominant or not.

The first group claims that it is, the second that it is not. There is no way we can yet resolve the problem because there are arguments for and against both sides. In the Venusian atmosphere, turbulent mixing has certainly stopped by 200 km altitude but the turbopause could be at virtually any height below 150 km. Both atomic oxygen and carbon monoxide have definitely been observed in the Martian upper atmosphere, but models of the Martian upper atmosphere based solely on CO$_2$ produce electron density profiles that fit the experimentally observed ones very well (fig. 7.3).

135

The first observations of the Martian ionosphere were conducted in 1965 by the American Mariner 4 space probe. The results showed that

(i) the maximum electron density in the daytime ionosphere of Mars at middle latitudes occurs at a height of 125 km and has an electron density in the range 9×10^{10} to 3×10^{11} m^{-3};

(ii) a small secondary maximum is observed at a height of about 20–25 km below the main maximum; and

(iii) the electron density of the night-time ionosphere of Mars does not exceed 10^{10} m^{-3}.

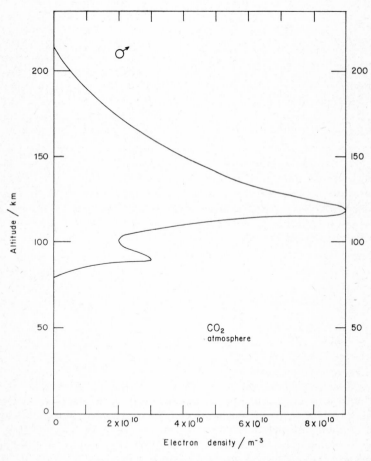

Fig. 7.3. The daytime ionosphere of Mars.

The Martian ionosphere is depicted in fig. 7.3. Its major features can be explained by theoretical models that treat it as a Chapman layer formed out of pure CO_2. The major peak in the ionosphere is due to the photoionization of CO_2 by the extreme ultraviolet radiation and the lower peak (which corresponds to the inflection in the Venusian ionosphere) is due to ionization of the CO_2 by X-rays. There are strong theoretical reasons for believing that cosmic rays will produce yet another smaller layer, equivalent to a D region, underneath the two layers of the Martian ionosphere. This layer should have an electron density between 10^8 and 10^{10} m^{-3} and have its peak in the 15 km to 40 km height range.

Like Venus, Mars does not have a magnetic field. Since Mars has an ionosphere with a charged particle density comparable to the ionosphere of Venus, we can expect a similar interaction between the solar wind and the planet in both cases. This means that we can expect a plasmapause on Mars somewhere above 400 km since the solar wind is weaker at the distance of Mars than at the distance of Venus.

The space probes to Mars up till now have not been equipped to look for either the plasmapause or the D region. We are going to have to wait a little longer to see if they really do exist.

7.4. *Jupiter*

The atmosphere of Jupiter, like the atmosphere of Venus, is dominated by clouds, though the cover on Jupiter is not as complete as it is on Venus. There seem to be two separate cloud systems on Jupiter—one composed of small particles of ammonia ice above one composed of normal water ice. In the temperature profile in fig. 7.1 I have assumed that the top of the water ice clouds marks the surface of the planet. This may be completely wrong. We do not even know whether Jupiter has a solid surface or a liquid surface.

We do know however that the interior of Jupiter, which is composed primarily of hydrogen, is very hot. This heat is accompanied by very great pressures so that the inside of Jupiter is composed of rotating ionized liquid hydrogen, and this plasma convection generates the magnetic field of Jupiter in much the same way that the Earth's molten core generates the Earth's magnetic field.

One of the few facts about Jupiter that we do know for certain is that it has a magnetic field. We know this because the high-energy particles trapped in the Jovian radiation belts emit radio waves from 5 MHz to 50 MHz known as decametric radiation, since its wavelength is tens of metres long.

The typical particle energies in Jupiter's radiation belts are about 50 times as great as the energies of the particles in the Earth's radiation belts and there are many more particles in the Jovian belts than in the terrestrial ones. The reason for this is that the magnetic field of Jupiter is 30 times greater than the Earth's. The energies of the particles are then greater by a somewhat larger factor. Because of this situation, the theory of the acceleration of these particles predicts an enormously greater flux of particles at any specified energy. Jupiter probably has wondrous aurorae!

The existence of these large numbers of very energetic particles produced a fierce controversy amongst scientists as to whether the Pioneer 10 spacecraft would survive its passage through the radiation belts. Some scientists said it would not, others insisted that it would. In December 1973 Pioneer 10 safely penetrated the radiation belts, to the joy of most of the scientific community. Apparently the moons of Jupiter, whilst orbiting through the radiation belts, modulate the radiation belts so that they are not as dangerous as they would be if Jupiter had no moons.

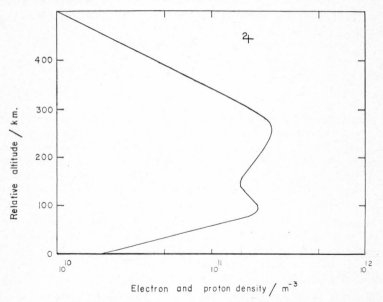

Fig. 7.4. A model for Jupiter's ionosphere. The altitude is relative since the position of the planet's surface is unknown.

Jupiter's atmosphere, like Jupiter's interior, is almost completely hydrogen. There is also some helium around and it is currently fashionable to use the same ratio of He to H_2 for Jupiter that is known to exist on the Sun—1 : 8. This has not produced any problems so far but then any ratio from 0 : 8 to 4 : 8 would be equally good. Like so much else about Jupiter—we just don't know. The minor constituents on Jupiter are ammonia NH_3, which is what the clouds are composed of, methane CH_4, and water H_2O. All of the planet's oxygen is contained in H_2O molecules, all its carbon in CH_4 and all its nitrogen in NH_3.

Though we have, as yet, no observational data on Jupiter's ionosphere, current models assume that the following reactions are dominant in producing ions and electrons.

$$hf + H_2 \rightarrow H_2^+ + e \rightarrow H^+ + H + e$$

$$e + H_2 \rightarrow H_2^+ + 2e \rightarrow H^+ + H + 2e$$

where hf represents ionizing radiation. Virtually all of Jupiter's ionosphere is expected to be protons, H^+, and electrons though it is possible that there may be H_3^+ ions and the complex HeH^+ ions present in small quantities.

A computed model for Jupiter's ionosphere is depicted in fig. 7.4. By the time you read this book, the data from the Jupiter fly-by missions will have been published and we shall know whether fig. 7.4 is a realistic model or whether it is as wildly wrong as were the early computed models of the Martian ionosphere. Preliminary results of Pioneer 11 reveal a peak electron density of $10^{11}\,m^{-3}$, at 67 000 km from the centre of the planet, with a temperature of 750 K for the layer.

Further reading

Planetary Meteorology

The book by Goody and Walker, mentioned in Chapter 1, includes simple discussions on planetary meteorology. An article at the same level as this book is:

Goody, Richard, 1973. Weather and the inner planets, *New Scientist*, **58,** 602–605.

Excellent but sophisticated reviews are:

Hunten, Donald M., 1971. Composition and structure of planetary atmospheres, *Space Science Reviews*, **12,** 539–599.
Newburn, R. L., Jr., and Gulkis, S., 1973. A survey of the outer planets, *Space Science Reviews*, **14,** 179–271.
Stone, Peter H., 1973. The dynamics of the atmospheres of the major planets, *Space Science Reviews*, **14,** 444–459.

Planetary Aeronomy

The book by Whitten and Poppoff, mentioned in Chapter 5, includes discussions on the aeronomy of the planets, scattered throughout the book.

More specialized reviews are:

Whitten, R. C., and Colin, L., 1974. The ionospheres of Mars and Venus, *Reviews of Geophysics and Space Physics*, **12,** 155–192.

McElroy, Michael B., 1973. The ionospheres of the major planets, *Space Science Reviews*, **14,** 460–473.

Kennel, C. F., 1973. Magnetospheres of the planets, *Space Science Reviews*, **14,** 511–533.

and the book:

Bauer, S. J., 1973. *Physics of Planetary Ionospheres.* (Berlin: Springer-Verlag.)

General

The Bulletin of the Atomic Scientists, *Science and Public Affairs* has carried excellent interviews conducted by Sally Jacobsen. These are at a simple general level with (amongst others):

Alfvén, Hannes, 1973. (On space exploration), **29,** No. 2, 30–32.

Parker, Eugene, 1973. (On the solar wind, magnetic fields and Earth weather), **29,** No. 5, 25–30.

Van Allen, James A., 1973. (On the trip to Jupiter), **29,** No. 10, 52–56.

I would also recommend the article by Garry Hunt, Pioneer 10: the preliminary results, *New Scientist*, 1974, **61,** 125–127.

APPENDIX

Satellites launched November and December, 1972

Name	Country	Launch date
Cosmos 528 to		
Cosmos 536	U.S.S.R.	1 November, 1972
USAF Metsat	U.S.A.	9 November, 1972
Anik 1	Canada	10 November, 1972
Explorer 48	U.S.A.	15 November, 1972
Esro 4	Europe	22 November, 1972
Cosmos 537	U.S.S.R.	25 November, 1972
Intercosmos 8	U.S.S.R.	30 November, 1972
Molniya 1X	U.S.S.R.	2 December, 1972
Nimbus 5	U.S.A.	11 December, 1972
Molniya 2D	U.S.S.R.	12 December, 1972
Cosmos 538	U.S.S.R.	14 December, 1972
Aeros	W. Germany	16 December, 1972
1972—101A	U.S.A.	20 December, 1972
Cosmos 539	U.S.S.R.	21 December, 1972
1972—103A	U.S.A.	21 December, 1972
Cosmos 540	U.S.S.R.	26 December, 1972
Cosmos 541	U.S.S.R.	27 December, 1972
Cosmos 542	U.S.S.R.	28 December, 1972

INDEX

THE WYKEHAM SCIENCE SERIES

THE WYKEHAM ENGINEERING AND TECHNOLOGY SERIES

All orders and requests for inspection copies should be sent to the appropriate agents. A list of agents and their territories is given on the verso of the title page of this book.

† (*Paper and Cloth Editions available.*)